IMPERIAL DEATH STAR

DS-1 Orbital Battle Station

Owner's Workshop Manual

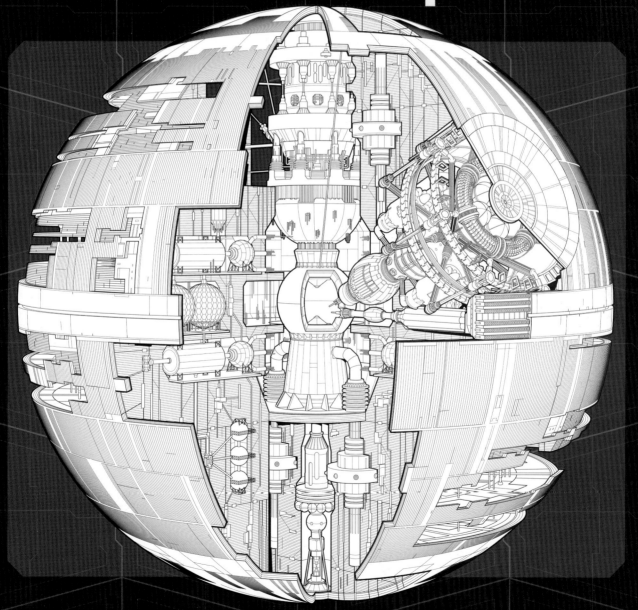

Ryder Windham

Chris Reiff and **Chris Trevas**

CONTENTS

↑ Imperial Schematic Design System data, obtained by a rebel agent from a military communications complex on Galvoni III after the Battle of Yavin, yielded schematics for a concept "Death Star" with a superlaser cannon located on the sphere's equator.

TO: His Imperial Majesty, Emperor Palpatine

FROM: Governor Tarkin, Seswenna Sector, Eriadu

REGARDING: Increasing the security of the Empire

▶ Your Majesty, it has long been my contention that your New Order needs one undeniable and overwhelming symbol to impress and, yes, frighten the masses. The average citizen has no grasp of numbers nor a head for calculation. I maintain that the effectiveness of the Star Destroyer stems from not only its massive firepower but also from its size. When citizens look at a Star Destroyer and then compare it to the craft which might be mustered to attack it, they have a tendency to dismiss such a notion as suicidal rather than approach the problem tactically.

This natural state can be exploited to a far greater degree, as the average citizen deals in symbols, not rational analysis. If we present the galaxy with a weapon so powerful, so immense as to defy all conceivable opposition against it, a weapon invulnerable and invincible in battle, then that weapon shall become the symbol of the Empire. We need only a handful, perhaps as few as one, of these weapons to subjugate a thousand worlds. It must have force enough to dispatch an entire system, power enough to shatter planets. The fear such a weapon will inspire will be great enough for you to rule the galaxy unchallenged. What do you need with the Senate when you can give direct control of territories to your hand-picked regional governors? Sweep away the last remnants of the Old Republic and let fear keep the local systems in line—fear of our ultimate weapon.

I am ready to begin work to implement these steps at your word.

#001044.92V

TO: Grand Moff Tarkin

FROM: Imperial Advisor Ars Dangor, for the Emperor

REGARDING: The Tarkin Doctrine

▶ You have read correctly, valued servant. Everything you have suggested will be implemented in a policy to be officially known as the Tarkin Doctrine. Rule through fear instead of through idealistic government agencies has a satisfying appeal to the Emperor. As such, the following title is bestowed upon you immediately, along with all relevant powers pertaining to such.

▶ You are now Grand Moff Tarkin, the first of a new order of Imperial officials.
▶ You have complete authority and control of Oversector Outer, which includes most of the sectors considered the Outer Rim Territories.
▶ You are to implement under extreme secrecy the design and construction of your ultimate tool of fear, code-named the Death Star Project.
▶ You have command of four Sector Groups to use to maintain the peace and to provide security for the Death Star Project.

The Emperor is pleased, Grand Moff Tarkin. Do not disappoint him.

#001044.92V

THE HISTORY OF THE DEATH STAR

Nearly three decades before the Battle of Yavin, starship engineer Raith Sienar conceived the Expeditionary Battle Planetoid, a one-hundred-kilometer sphere with a smaller sphere at each pole, a large turbolaser at its core, and the capability to destroy an entire planet. Realizing that such a weapon would require a huge implosion core for power as well as great advances in hypermatter technology, Sienar dismissed his own concept as impractical.

Despite his misgivings, Sienar presented his concept for the Expeditionary Battle Planetoid to his friend, Republic Outland Regions Security Force Commander Wilhuff Tarkin, a native or Eriadu. Tarkin believed the concept had potential, and after he entered a career in politics and became the lieutenant governor of Eriadu, he conveyed his strong interest in the weapon to the Republic's leader, Supreme Chancellor Palaptine.

Palpatine assigned engineer and architect Bevel Lemelisk to pursue the necessary advances in hypermatter science. As the battle station project shifted from conceptual stage to architectural planning, work moved to the planet Geonosis, where Lemelisk teamed with the hive-minded Geonosians to hammer out structural and power supply issues. The weapon's schematics were in a laboratory on Geonosis when the Geonosians joined the Separatist movement, which represented numerous worlds that wanted to secede from the Galactic Republic. The Separatist leader Count Dooku, a former Jedi, absconded with the schematics during the battle that launched the Clone Wars.

Although Palpatine and Dooku led the opposing factions in the Clone Wars, both men were actually Sith Lords and allies. It remains unknown whether Wilhuff Tarkin—who served as a Republic Navy officer in the Clone Wars—was aware that either man was a Sith Lord. Following the Clone Wars, Palpatine and Tarkin continued working on the code-named Death Star project in secret, their goal to create a weapon that would permanently silence all who dared to resist Imperial rule.

Tarkin oversaw construction of the 120km-diameter Death Star in the Horuz system, in orbit of the prison world of Despayre. Supply and labor issues, unexpected technical difficulties, and acts of sabotage delayed the project for years. When construction was finished, the Death Star's laser targeted Despayre, and reduced it to asteroidal dust. Members of the Rebel Alliance stole the superweapon's schematics, and delivered them to technicians at the rebel base on Yavin 4, but not before the Death Star also destroyed the planet Alderaan.

With little doubt that the Empire's next target would be Yavin 4, the rebels raced to find any strategic vulnerability in the weapon's design. They found a flaw, an unshielded thermal exhaust vent, and the rebel pilot Luke Skywalker was able to destroy the Death Star by firing proton torpedoes into the vent.

Four years later, the rebels discovered the existence of a second Death Star that was still under construction in the Endor system. More than a weapon of terror, this Death Star was part of an elaborate trap, as the Empire knew the rebels would be unable to resist mounting an assault. Despite incredible odds, the rebels managed to first destroy the shield generator that protected the Death Star, and then the battle station itself. Within a month after the Battle of Endor, Rebel Alliance leader Mon Mothma declared the end of the rebellion and the birth of the New Republic.

Today, the Death Star remains a symbol of the Empire's oppression but also represents the Empire's greatest weakness: the belief that technology was supreme, and all foes insignificant.

Imperial TIE fighters patrol the orbit of the under-construction Death Star.

TRADE FEDERATION BATTLESHIP

During the early stages of transforming Raith Sienar's concepts for the Expeditionary Battle Planetoid into an actual superweapon, Bevel Lemelisk's team of engineers drew inspiration from the *Lucrehulk*-class cargo freighters that the Trade Federation had converted into battleships.

Originally manufactured by Hoersch-Kessel Drive, the *Lucrehulk* is over three kilometers in diameter, and resembles a flattened disc that forms a split ring around a central sphere. The ring is split at the front of the craft, revealing two mammoth docking bays lined with forward docking claws. The ring also houses cavernous hangar bays, which were cargo holds in the ship's previous freighter configuration. The sphere contains the ship's massive computer and multiple power systems, and a compact hypermatter-annihilation reactor. A tower on the sphere houses a spacious command bridge; on *Lucrehulk*-class LH-3210 Cargo Haulers converted to serve as control ships for the Trade Federation's droid armies, a military control tower was also installed.

Although the *Lucrehulk* is an extremely powerful vessel, the conversion from freighter to warship was not entirely effective. The reactor-support assemblies retained independent fusion-powered triggers and confinement-field generators for the hypermatter main reactors, and were extremely volatile. The addition of retractable turbolasers along the equator of the ship left large blind spots that enemy starfighters could exploit by flying close to the hull.

← The Trade Federation used their battleships to blockade worlds they sought to conquer, but the warships were vulnerable to attack by small starfighters.

SPECIFICATIONS

CRAFT: *Lucrehulk*-class Battleship (converted freighter)
MANUFACTURER: Hoersch-Kessel Drive Inc. (primary contractor)
DIAMETER: 3,170m (10,400ft)
SUBLIGHT ENGINES: Rendili stardrive proton 2 (primary); proton 12 (secondary)
HYPERDRIVE: Class 2
HYPERDRIVE BACKUP: Class 10
SHIELDING: Equipped

NAVIGATION SYSTEM: Navicomputer
ARMAMENT: 42 quad laser emplacements
CREW: 25 (command staff)
PASSENGERS: 139,000 battle droids
CARGO: 500 million tons
CONSUMABLES: 500 days
COST: Not for sale (black market value 40,000,000)

TRADE FEDERATION CORE SHIP

After the Battle of Naboo, the Republic Senate ordered the Trade Federation to dissolve its army and disassemble its battleships. The Trade Federation pretended to comply but instead converted the central spheres into detachable core ships, which were engineered for planetary landings and equipped with land and air defenses. Used at the Battle of Geonosis and throughout the Clone Wars, the core ships were serviced in special landing pits on planets affiliated to the Trade Federation. The pits were lined with gravitational reflectors, which assisted the core ship's repulsors, and enabled the ships to retreat into space and reattach to the hyperdrive-equipped outer rings. Following the Clone Wars, most of the few remaining Trade Federation battleships and core ships wound up in the Corporate Sector.

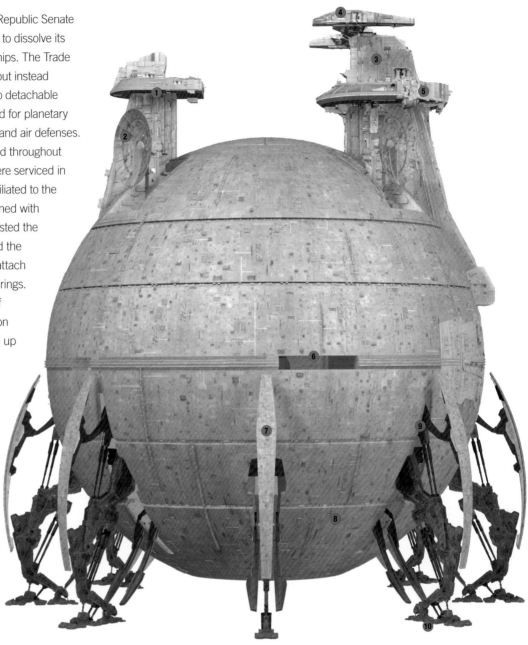

1. Forward control tower
2. Droid-feedback rectenna
3. Command bridge tower
4. Scanner array
5. Docking ring
6. Equatorial bay
7. Hull section covers
8. Repulsorlift suspensors
9. Landing gear retractors
10. Foot pads

SPECIFICATIONS

CRAFT: Trade Federation Core Ship
MANUFACTURER: Hoersch-Kessel Drive Inc. (basic Core Ship); Baktoid Combat Automata (droid-army control core)
DIAMETER: 696m (2285ft)
HYPERDRIVE: None
HYPERDRIVE BACKUP: None
SHIELDING: Equipped
NAVIGATION SYSTEM: Navicomputer

ARMAMENT: 280 point-defense light laser cannons
CREW: 60 Trade Federation supervisors; 3,000 Droid Crew; 200,000 maintenance droids
PASSENGERS: stateroom capacity for 60,000 trade representatives
CARGO: approx. 66 million tons
CONSUMABLES: 300 days
COST: Not for sale (black market value 25,000,000)

Although the Jedi Order was decimated in the purge that concluded the Clone Wars, dozens of Jedi younglings managed to take refuge at a Jedi enclave that had been established decades earlier on the planet Belsavis. The enclave lay in the Plawal rift, a series of geothermal-heated valleys that rested between wind-scoured glaciers, and was protected from above by an immense transparisteel dome. Soon after the Jedi purge, Emperor Palpatine secretly ordered the construction of an automated "battlemoon", its singular goal to wipe out the surviving Jedi on Belsavis. The battlemoon was named the *Eye of Palpatine*.

According to reconstructed Imperial documents, Palpatine specifically indicated that the battlemoon should resemble an asteroid, complete with impact craters, and he maintained such camouflage was necessary to deceive or baffle sensor scans from enemy worlds and vessels. However, given that the Death Star project was already in the works when Palpatine issued the order to build his battlemoon, historians have theorized that the Emperor was less interested in creating a natural-looking superweapon than he was intent on keeping secrecy, and hesitant to reveal the grandness of his evil ambitions so early in his rule. Had he blatantly promoted his intent to wipe out every inhabitant in the Plawal rift, most of whom were children, his actions would have caused untold outrage in the Senate.

Imperial engineer Ohran Keldor designed the battlemoon, which was constructed at the shipyards of Rothana and also Patriim. Keldor utilized an asteroid from the Patriim system as a source of raw materials as well as a foundation upon which he installed huge engines and turbolaser cannons. The result was a 19,000-meter-long weapon, paid for by government funds that had been diverted by Palpatine himself. To further maintain secrecy, Palpatine also arranged for the *Eye* to pick up contingents of stormtroopers on various worlds throughout the Outer Rim.

Despite the Emperor's schemes, two Jedi sabotaged the *Eye of Palpatine*, and brought it to a stop before it ever picked up the waiting stormtroopers. The inhabitants of Belsavis escaped, and the furious Emperor imprisoned many of those responsible for losing the *Eye*. For nearly three decades, the *Eye* remained dormant amidst the asteroids in the Moonflower Nebula in the Wild Space region of the galaxy. Eight years after the Battle of Endor, Luke Skywalker and two of his Jedi students discovered the battlemoon, and worked together to destroy it.

⬇ With its rocky, cratered surface, the *Eye of Palpatine* remained unnoticed for decades in an asteroid belt in the Moonflower Nebula.

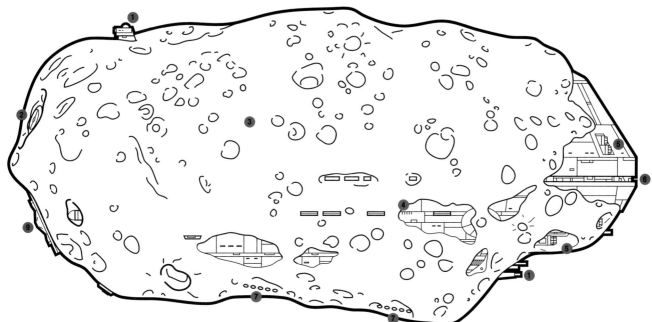

1. Deflector shield generator
2. Sensor arrays
3. Hollowed asteroid shell
4. Hangar bays
5. Sublight engines
6. Hyperdrive
7. Ventral turbolaser batteries
8. Main bridge
9. Laser targeting beam emitter
10. Forward focused turbolaser batteries

⬇ Palpatine, Emperor of the Galactic Empire.

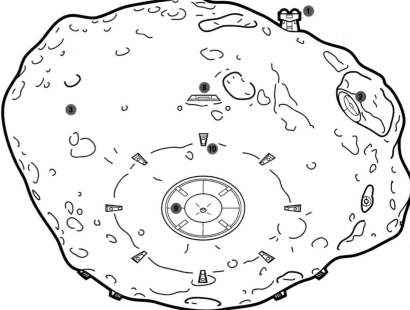

SPECIFICATIONS

CRAFT: Eye of Palpatine
TYPE: Automated battlemoon
MANUFACTURER: Rothana Heavy Engineering
LENGTH: 19,000m
HYPERDRIVE: Class 5
HYPERDRIVE BACKUP: Class 20
SHIELDING: Merr-Sonn *Guardian*-class shield generators

NAVIGATION SYSTEM: Advanced AI Navicomputer
ARMAMENT: Turbolaser cannons
CREW: Unmanned
PASSENGERS: Imperial stormtroopers
CARGO CAPACITY: Unknown
CONSUMABLES: 90 days (estimated)
COST: Unknown

TORPEDO SPHERE

A dedicated siege platform produced for the Empire by Loronar Defense Industries, the Torpedo Sphere is designed for the singular purpose of disabling planetary defense shields. The primary armament of a Torpedo Sphere is an assembly of 500 proton torpedo tubes. The tubes are arranged in an inverted conical formation, a design that enables all torpedo-launchers to fire simultaneously at one target. The tubes are circled by ten heavy turbolaser batteries.

The Torpedo Sphere is covered in thousands of dedicated energy receptors (DERs) designed to analyze energy shield emissions. Planetary shields are never uniformly even and experience power anomalies and fluctuations. To make an assault, the Torpedo Sphere arrives in a planet's orbit, and then trains its DERs to search for weak points in the planet's shielding. These weak points rarely show a power drop of more than 20 percent, and rarely larger than a six-meter square, but are nevertheless sufficiently vulnerable areas. The Torpedo Sphere's sensors cannot penetrate full planetary shields, so the only way the Sphere's crew can determine the location of a planet's shield generators is to study the power waves and seek their initial source.

Because a station the size of a Torpedo Sphere cannot fire-link weapons, the torpedo tubes must be carefully coordinated by more than 100 heavy-weapons technicians. The process for determining the location of a planetary shield's weak point and calculating an attack on that specific point can take hours. This time-consuming process precludes the possibility to fire the tubes together at anything more mobile than a planet. Although it is possible to take some fire-links off the normal weapon control system and fire normally at starship-sized targets, only fifty tubes can be managed at a time in this manner.

Once the weak points in a shield have been found, the technicians fire the proton torpedos in unison at one weak point. This action is followed with a barrage of turbolaser blasts directed at the planetary defense generators. Planetary defense shields are rarely disabled for more than a few microseconds, so if the first barrage does not shatter the shield, the process must start all over again.

The siege platform's ovoid-shape and considerable firepower have encouraged some Imperial officers to liken the Torpedo Sphere to a "miniature Death Star." While the Torpedo Sphere is hardly capable of destroying a planet, it is a formidable weapon. Six Torpedo Spheres are currently in service.

⬇ Although the Empire maintained control of all Torpedo Spheres, Emperor Palpatine blanketed the planet Coruscant with powerful shield generators that were engineered to withstand an orbital bombardment of proton torpedoes.

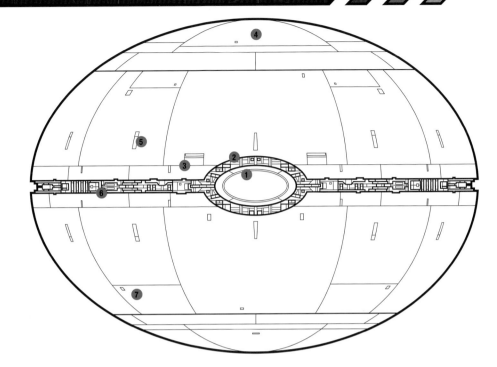

1. Torpedo tube array
2. Turbolaser batteries
3. Deflector shield generator
4. Main bridge
5. Dedicated energy receptors
6. Hangar bays
7. Sensor arrays
8. Sublight engines
9. Hyperdrive

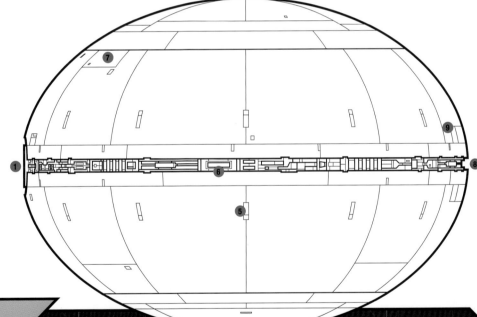

SPECIFICATIONS

CRAFT: Loronar's Torpedo Sphere
TYPE: Dedicated siege platform
MANUFACTURER: Loronar Defense Industries
LENGTH: 1,900m
HYPERDRIVE: Class 3
HYPERDRIVE BACKUP: Class 18
SHIELDING: Loronar DS-13 projectors
NAVIGATION SYSTEM: Sienar Fleet Systems navicomputer

ARMAMENT: 10 turbolaser batteries; 500 proton torpedo tubes
CREW: 61,245 gunners; 2,030 skeleton
PASSENGERS: 8,540 (troops)
CARGO CAPACITY: Unknown
CONSUMABLES: 4 years
COST: Not for sale (construction cost unknown)

THE TARKIN

Although the Rebel Alliance claimed victory at the Battle at Yavin, the era of the Death Stars was far from over. Emperor Palpatine had already ordered the construction of a second Death Star, and was also manufacturing a pair of mammoth warships—*Eclipse*-class Super Star Destroyers—at Kuat and Byss. To test the technology of the *Eclipse*-class's ship-mounted superlasers, and also to divert the Alliance's attention from the second Death Star, the Emperor assigned Bevel Lemelisk to develop a prototype of the *Eclipse*-class into an operational weapon that would also serve as a test bed for new

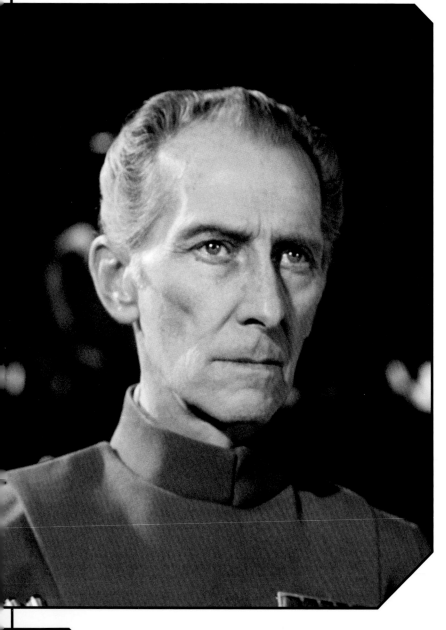

⬇ Grand Moff Tarkin aboard the Death Star. Both the Death Star and the Tarkin were paid for by funds diverted from the Departments of System Exploration and Public Works.

technology. The result was the *Tarkin,* named in honor of the martyred Grand Moff Tarkin.

Most of the members of Lemelisk's design team were unaware of the fact that their assignment was to build a prototype, and were led to believe that the *Tarkin* was intended as an official Imperial battle station. They replicated the Death Star's main offensive battery, the ionic cannon superlaser, and essentially bracketed the weapon with a set of giant engines and defensive shield generators. Not surprisingly, the design team did not leave any thermal exhaust ports exposed, effectively removing the flaw that had allowed the Rebel Alliance to destroy the first Death Star.

The *Tarkin* was built in secret at a dry dock in orbit of the garrison planet Hockaleg in the Patriim system, and construction was overseen by Imperial Admiral Nod Warfield. The prototype's superlaser came to the attention of Imperial Grand Admiral Martio Batch, who had been assigned by the Emperor to develop cloaking technologies. Although cloaking devices for starships had once been common, the technology had become virtually obsolete since the mines of Aeten II, an Outer Rim world in the Dreighton Nebula, had been depleted of the rare stygium crystals required for the devices. Batch diverted the *Tarkin* to Aeten II and used the prototype's superlaser to shatter the entire world, which released thousands of stygium crystals that were subsequently collected by Batch's forces.

After the *Tarkin* returned to Hockaleg's orbit for additional modifications and further testing, a Rebel Alliance officer, Captain Maraba Tev, was on a high-risk spy mission in the Patriim system when he discovered the Empire's secret weapon. Tev managed to obtain the *Tarkin*'s schematics, which enabled a rebel assault squad to infiltrate the enormous vessel. The assault squad included Princess Leia Organa, who sabotaged the ionic cannon's activation mechanism by switching two wires to reverse the polarity modes of the cannon's fire controls. After the squad escaped the *Tarkin*, the Imperials attempted to fire their superlaser at the squad's ship, but Leia's sabotage made the cannon fire on itself, causing the *Tarkin* to self-destruct.

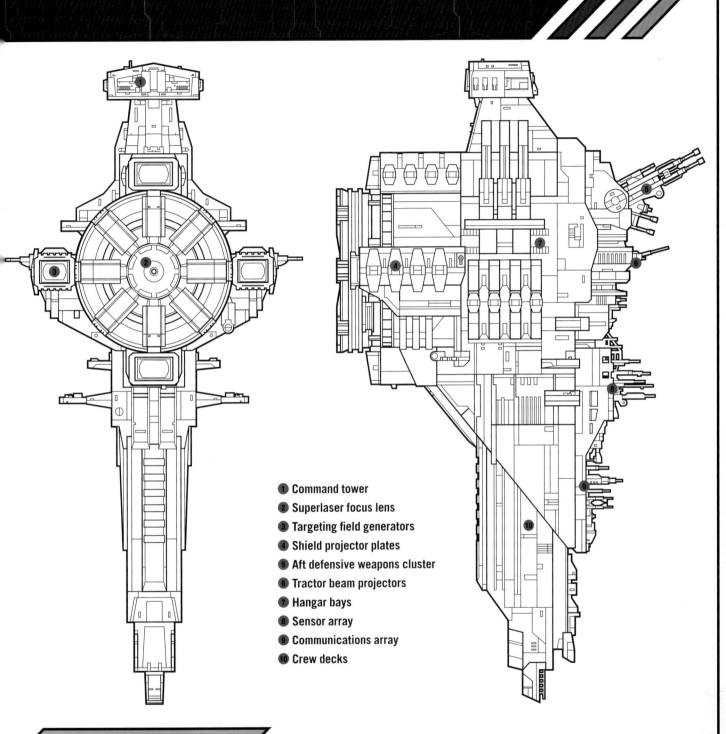

1 **Command tower**
2 **Superlaser focus lens**
3 **Targeting field generators**
4 **Shield projector plates**
5 **Aft defensive weapons cluster**
6 **Tractor beam projectors**
7 **Hangar bays**
8 **Sensor array**
9 **Communications array**
10 **Crew decks**

SPECIFICATIONS

CRAFT: **The Tarkin**
TYPE: **Battlestation**
MANUFACTURER: **Imperial Department of Military Research**
LENGTH: **42km**
HEIGHT: **70km**
HYPERDRIVE: **Class 4**
HYPERDRIVE BACKUP: **Class 20**

SHIELDING: **Borstel Galactic Defense field generators**
NAVIGATION SYSTEM: **Sienar Fleet Systems navicomputer**
ARMAMENT: **Superlaser**
CREW: **43,863 (35,705 operational staff, 8,158 gunners)**
PASSENGERS: **105,417**
CONSUMABLES: **2 years (estimated)**
COST: **Unknown**

GRAND MOFF TARKIN

A native of Eriadu, Wilhuff Tarkin graduated from the Academy, joined the Republic Outland Regions Security Force, and quickly gained a reputation for quelling piracy around Eriadu and other Rim worlds. He reached the rank of commander before retiring, then entered politics and became lieutenant governor of Eriadu. When Senator Palpatine was elected to the office of Supreme Chancellor, Tarkin realized a major political shift had occurred, and he insinuated himself to become recognized as one of Palpatine's most ardent supporters.

Tarkin befriended the engineer Raith Sienar, who described his idea for an "expeditionary battle planetoid". Tarkin eventually relayed the idea to Palpatine, who was intrigued. During the Clone Wars, Tarkin served as the Seswenna sector's governor. After Palpatine became Emperor, he appointed Tarkin as the Galactic Empire's first sector governor, which carried the designation Moff.

Tarkin formulated what became known as the Tarkin Doctrine. Officially known as Imperial Communiqué #001044.92v, the Doctrine consisted of Tarkin's plans for increasing security and maintaining order within the Empire. His plans included the proposal for "*a weapon so powerful, so immense as to defy all conceivable opposition against it*", which would be used to "*rule through the fear of force rather than through force itself*".

Palpatine subsequently appointed Tarkin as the first Grand Moff, and gave him oversight of the construction of Sienar's conceived superweapon, which was dubbed the Death Star.

RAITH SIENAR

BEVEL LEMELISK

Born into a family of wealthy industrialists, Raith Sienar trained at the Rigovian Technical University, and became an engineer and hyperspace explorer. He mapped dozens of new hyperspace lanes, discovered exploitable systems in the Unknown Regions, and amassed his own fortune by the age of 20.

He founded Sienar Design Systems as well as its clandestine division, Advanced Projects Laboratory, and specialized in one-of-a-kind contracts, designing starships for wealthy clients. Eventually, he became CEO of his family's most profitable company, Sienar Technologies. An innovative and by all accounts brilliant engineer, Sienar frequently drew inspiration from mistakes made by others. He invested heavily in the scrapped projects of his competitors and searched the designs for new ideas that had failed for simple reasons, and which could be corrected to serve his own purposes, such as transforming stock vessels into fast, unique starships. He pushed ion-drive technology to its limits, and produced the first Twin Ion Drive (T.I.E.) starfighter.

Sienar's longtime friend Wilhuff Tarkin ensured Sienar Technologies secured numerous contracts with the Republic for Sienar's companies. After Palpatine became Emperor, Sienar nationalized Sienar Technologies, and gave the company a new name: Sienar Fleet Systems. His T.I.E. design was utilized for the Imperial TIE fighter, TIE bomber, infiltrator, Advanced, and other TIE variants.

← Grand Moff Tarkin in uniform, shortly after the end of the Clone Wars.

An engineer and architect, Bevel Lemelisk studied under Nasdra Magrody, founder of the Magrody Institute of Programmable Intelligence. During the Clone Wars, he worked with the esteemed engineer Walex Blissex, and assisted Blissex in designing the *Victory*-class Star Destroyer for the Grand Army of the Republic. After Palpatine declared himself Emperor, Grand Moff Tarkin assigned Lemelisk to the Maw Installation, where he became chief engineer of the Death Star project.

As chief engineer, Lemelisk essentially outranked everyone affiliated with the Death Star's construction except for Tarkin. Along with Imperial scientist Frap Radicon and weapons engineer Umak Leth, he spent years working on the secret weapon. Lemelisk also discreetly enlisted the help of the Twi'lek scientist Tol Sivron, who conducted his research in a laboratory on his homeworld Ryloth. However, to maintain secrecy, Lemelisk deliberately gave limited data to Sivron, preventing him from knowing that he was working on a superweapon. At some point, Lemelisk was appointed Master of Imperial Projects. After completing the Death Star, he was assigned to work on Torpedo Spheres.

Despite Lemelisk's many contributions to the Empire, Emperor Palpatine held him personally responsible for the design flaw that enabled the Rebel Alliance to destroy the Death Star. According to various reports, Lemelisk attempted to flee Imperial authorities but was eventually captured and executed. However, other reports suggest that Palpatine—after the Battle of Yavin—assigned Lemelisk to oversee construction of the *Tarkin*. Rumors persist that Palpatine considered Lemelisk too valuable to kill, and opted to torture the engineer instead. Whether dead or alive, Lemelisk's current whereabouts remain unknown.

DEATH STAR PROTOTYPE

↑ Inside the Geonosian War Room on Geonosis, the Death Star plans appeared finished, but technical difficulties required Imperials to build a working prototype.

By the time Moff Tarkin had been promoted to Grand Moff Tarkin, numerous flaws in the original Geonosian plans for the Death Star battle station, as well as intelligence leaks and scattered efforts at sabotage, had led to ongoing construction delays. As the Imperial engineers continued to have great difficulty in adapting the Geonosian plans into a working model, Tarkin ordered a think tank of engineers to review the schematics for feasibility from top to bottom and create a working prototype Death Star.

For the prototype's construction, Tarkin also founded and selected the location of a top-secret research facility, built within and amidst linked asteroids inside a hidden island of gravitational stability in the exact center of the Maw black-hole cluster near Kessel. Eventually, the Twi-lek administrator Tol Sivron came to run Tarkin's Maw Installation, which was guarded by four Star Destroyers under the command of Admiral Natasi Daala.

Many proof-of-concept components, theoretical models, and performance tests were undertaken to hone the Death Star design. Work crews of Wookiee slaves assembled a scaled-down version of the core

SPECIFICATIONS

CRAFT: **Death Star Prototype**
TYPE: **Battlestation**
MANUFACTURER: **Imperial Department of Military Research**
LENGTH/WIDTH/HEIGHT: **120 kilometers**
HYPERDRIVE: **None**
HYPERDRIVE BACKUP: **None**
ENGINE UNITS: **Ion engines (for sublight travel only)**
SHIELDING: **Borstel Galactic Defense field generators**

NAVIGATION SYSTEM: **Interplanetary navicomputer**
CREW: **258**
PASSENGERS: **Stormtroopers and gunners**
CARGO CAPACITY: **Unknown**
CONSUMABLES: **2 months**
COST: **Unknown**

superlaser, which was mounted inside a stripped-down superstructure, an armillary sphere with a diameter of 120 kilometers. Because the prototype was never intended to be a practical weapon of war, the designers had no need to install maintenance and repair machinery, an immense computer core, or the enormous hyperdrive engines that were necessary for the full-scale Death Star. The only visible components inside the prototype's sphere were the giant reactor core, engines for sublight travel, and the prototype superlaser itself. A small command cabin with slave-rigged computer systems controlled the superlaser and drive units, and also minimized personnel requirements.

Compared with the working model of the first Death Star, the prototype superlaser had several disadvantages. The targeting system was never perfected, and the superlaser was incredibly wasteful of power, its storable batteries requiring several hours to recharge fully. Although the superlaser could be fired at reduced power, its destructive ability was reduced significantly. Firepower was only sufficient to destroy a planet's core and render the planet uninhabitable, but could not completely vaporize the targeted world.

The prototype proved effective, and construction resumed on the full-scale Death Star, which had been relocated to the Horuz system. Eleven years after the Death Star's destruction at Yavin, the prototype was still in orbit of the asteroid laboratories of the Maw Installation, and still guarded by Admiral Daala's forces, when New Republic agents, including Kyp Duron, discovered the superweapon at the secret facility. Kyp Duron subsequently managed to destroy the prototype by luring it into the Maw's black hole.

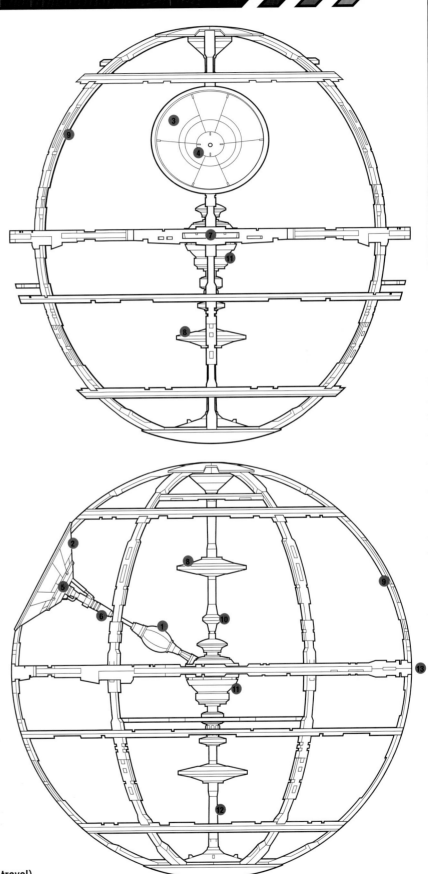

1. **Power amplification system**
2. **Focus lens frame**
3. **Superlaser focus lens**
4. **Amplification crystal prototype**
5. **Laser crystal**
6. **Superlaser power distribution shaft**
7. **Command cabin**
8. **Reactor core**
9. **Frame**
10. **Power cell coupling**
11. **Main reactor**
12. **Power distribution shaft**
13. **Ion engines (for sublight travel)**

DEATH STAR

To: Major Arhul Hextrophon, Executive Secretary and Master Historian, Alliance High Command
From: Lieutenant Voren Na'al, Assistant Historian
Regarding: Revised summary for the Death Star battle station

Although the conception and development of the Death Star occurred years before the Republic fell to Palpatine's Empire, there is little doubt that Palpatine knew such a superweapon would be vital to his goal to rule thousands of worlds. Because he was determined to gain respect as well as inspire fear throughout the galaxy, the Emperor demanded that the Death Star would defy all planetary defenses, and have the ability to destroy an entire world with one devastating stroke.

An equatorial trench divided the Death Star into two hemispheres, each of which was subdivided into 12 bridge-controlled zones for a total of 24 zones. Each zone was similar to a sub-batttle station, and had its own food replicators, hangar bays, detention blocks, medical centers, armories, and command centers. The upper hemisphere housed the superlaser, and all Imperial estimates indicated that a single blast would equal the combined firepower of the entire Imperial fleet.

The station's surface was covered with thousands of 'city sprawls', manned stations dedicated primarily to defense. These sprawls housed the majority of the Death Star's shield projectors and communications arrays. Most of the station's 'habitable' areas were on the surface or within the two to four kilometer thick crust. All of the 'below surface' facilities within the crust were considered part of the city sprawl. All data gathered by the clusters' sensors and manned stations were relayed to each zone's respective bridge, which was in turn relayed to the overbridge, a vast command center that constantly monitored all the work stations and datafiles on the battle station.

At the Death Star's core was an immense, cavernous housing for the battle station's power matrix. A fusion reactor, fed by stellar fuel bottles that lined its periphery, produced the raw energy demanded by the Death Star's superlaser. The reactor core, sublight and hyperdrive systems, and the superlaser housing filled approximately half of the battle station's interior. Sublight propulsion systems and defense field generators lined the outer equatorial regions.

When the first Death Star's construction was finished, it was the single largest object ever built.

↑Although the Death Star was equipped with mooring platforms for Imperial Star Destroyers, ship-to-ship transfers were typically made via shuttles.

↓ Arriving upon the Death Star in the Alderaan system, the crew of the YT-1300 freighter *Millennium Falcon* initially mistook the battle station for a small moon.

↑ 35 kilometers in diameter, the superlaser focus dish was the Death Star's most prominent surface feature.

SPECIFICATIONS

CRAFT: **Mk. 1 deep-space mobile battle station**
MANUFACTURER: **Imperial Department of Military Research/Sienar Fleet Systems**
DIAMETER: **120km (74.6 miles)**
HYPERDRIVE: **Class 4**
HYPERDRIVE BACKUP: **Class 20**
SHIELDING: **Equipped**
NAVIGATION SYSTEM: **Navicomputer**

ARMAMENT: **1 superlaser, 15,000 Taim & Bak D6 turbolaser batteries, 2,500 Borstel Galactic Defense SB-920 laser cannons, 2,500 Borstel MS-1 ion cannons, 768 Phylon tractor-beam emplacements, 11,000 combat vehicles**
CREW: **342,953 (285,675 operational staff, 57,278 gunners)**
PASSENGERS: **843,342**
CARGO CAPACITY: **Over one million kilotons**
CONSUMABLES: **3 years**
COST: **Unknown**

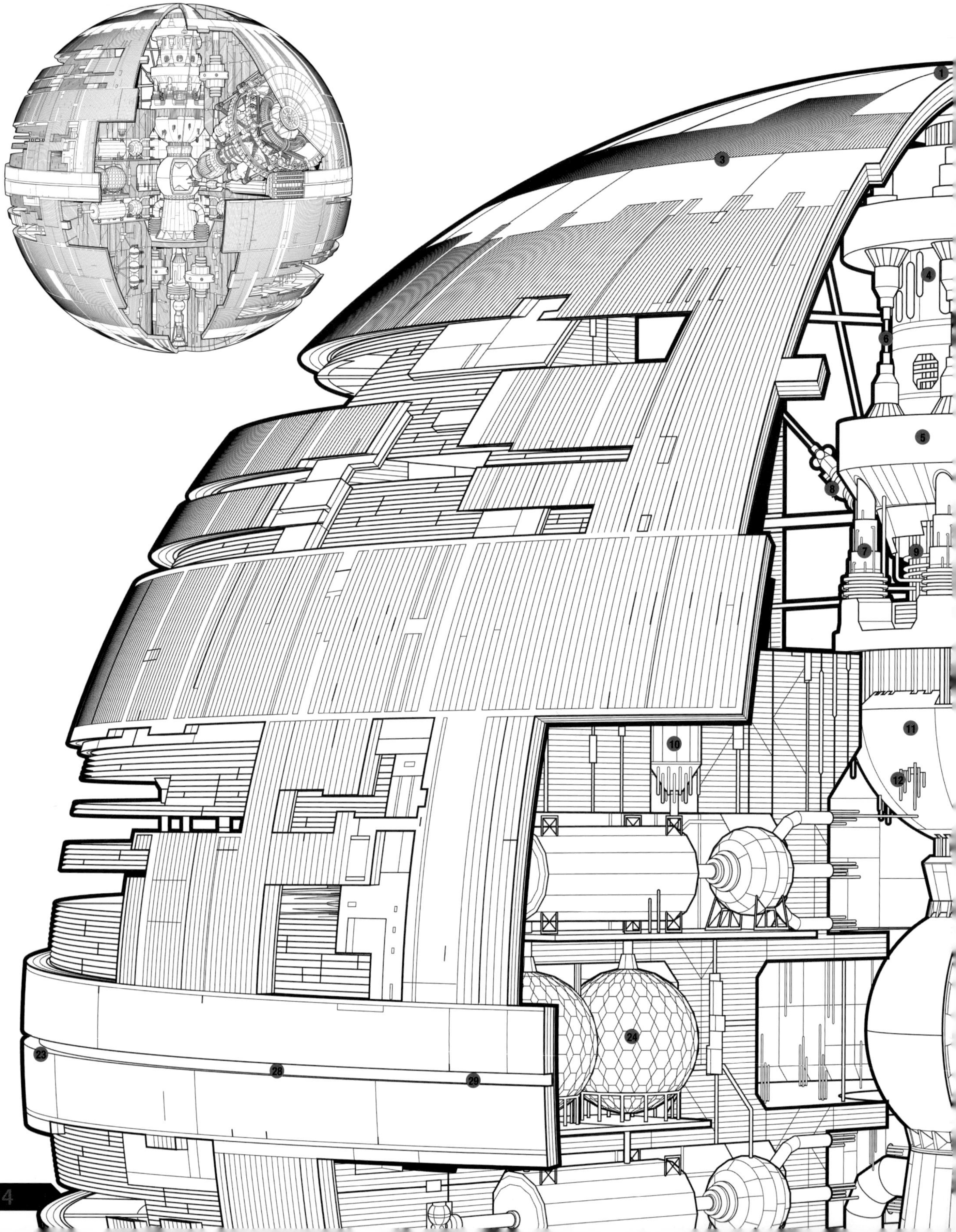
1
3
4
6
5
8
7
9
10
11
12
24
23
28
29

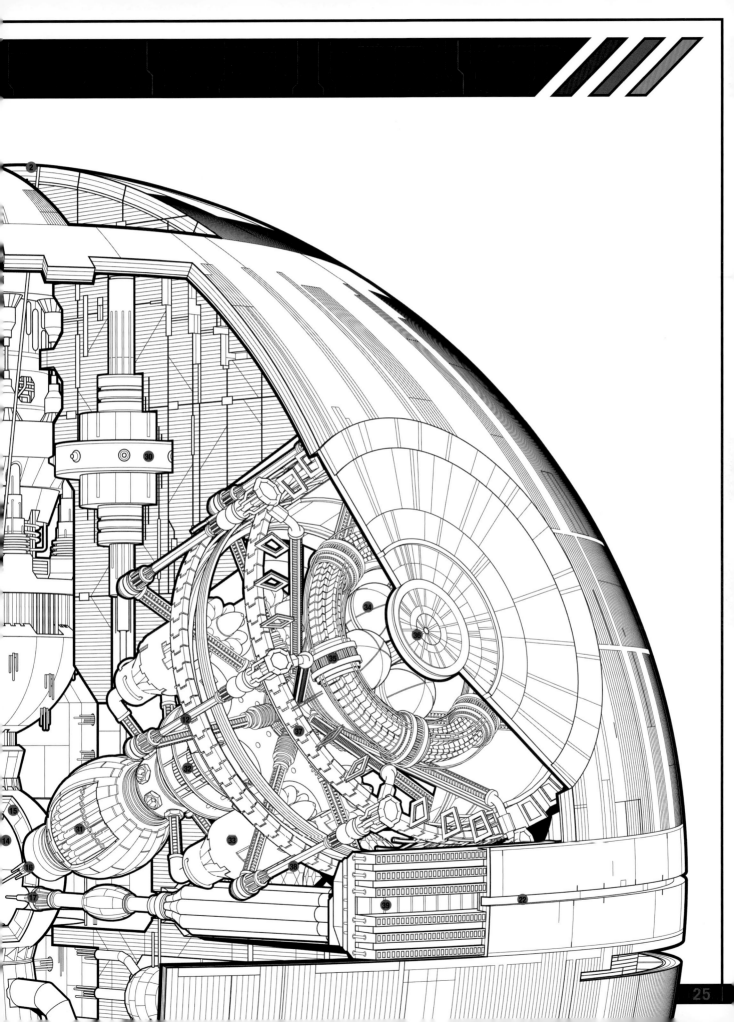

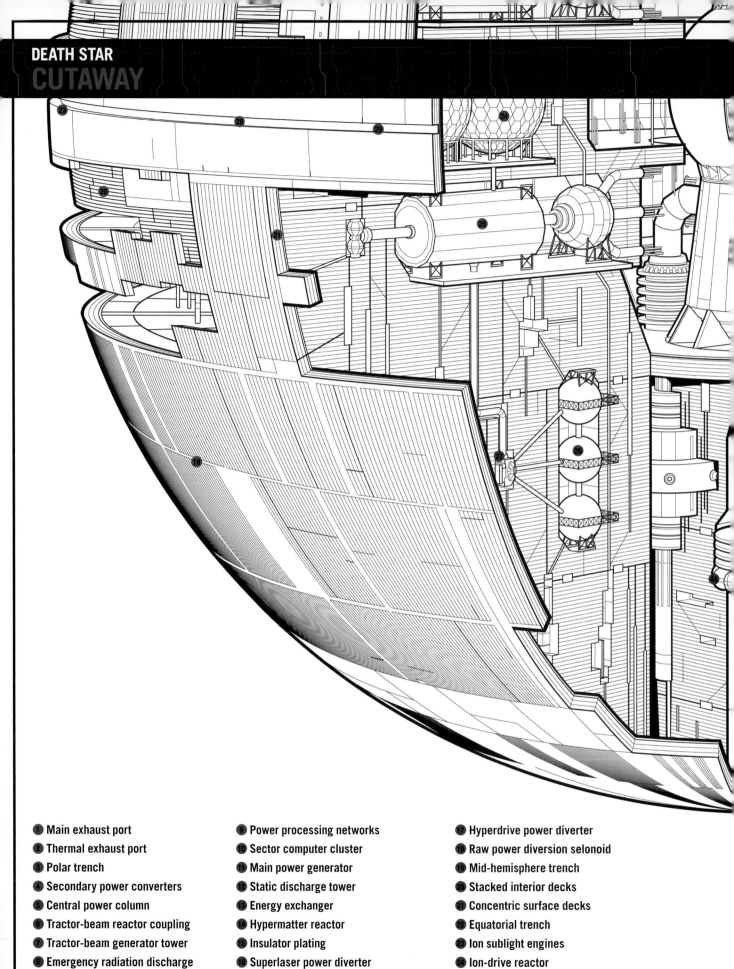

1. Main exhaust port
2. Thermal exhaust port
3. Polar trench
4. Secondary power converters
5. Central power column
6. Tractor-beam reactor coupling
7. Tractor-beam generator tower
8. Emergency radiation discharge
9. Power processing networks
10. Sector computer cluster
11. Main power generator
12. Static discharge tower
13. Energy exchanger
14. Hypermatter reactor
15. Insulator plating
16. Superlaser power diverter
17. Hyperdrive power diverter
18. Raw power diversion selonoid
19. Mid-hemisphere trench
20. Stacked interior decks
21. Concentric surface decks
22. Equatorial trench
23. Ion sublight engines
24. Ion-drive reactor

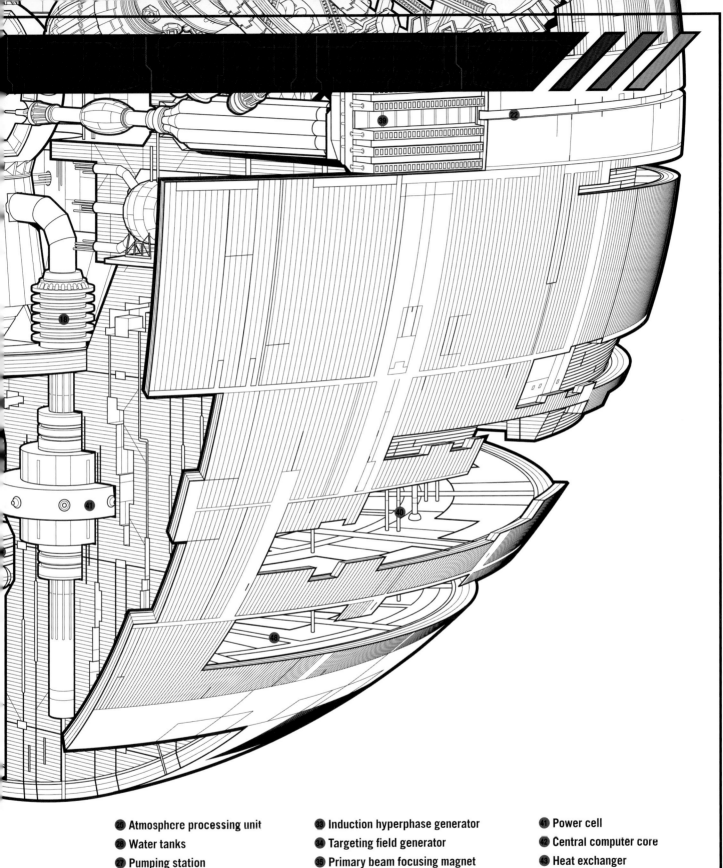

20 Atmosphere processing unit
26 Water tanks
27 Pumping station
28 Equatorial docking bay
29 Hangar bays
30 Superlaser power cell
31 Primary power amplifier
32 Firing field amplifier

33 Induction hyperphase generator
34 Targeting field generator
35 Primary beam focusing magnet
36 Carrier beam crystal
37 Magnetic shielding
38 Superlaser tributary beam shaft
39 Hyperdrive
40 Turbolift shafts

41 Power cell
42 Central computer core
43 Heat exchanger
44 Stellar fuel bottles
45 Cooling system
46 Refinery
47 Fuel collector
48 Superstructure

DEATH STAR
ELEVATION PLAN

1. Main exhaust port
2. Thermal exhaust port
3. Secondary power converters
4. Central power column
5. Tractor-beam reactor coupling
6. Tractor-beam generator tower
7. Emergency radiation discharge
8. Main power generator
9. Hypermatter reactor
10. Concentric surface decks
11. Ion sublight engines
12. Ion-drive reactor
13. Atmosphere processing unit
14. Water tanks
15. Overbridge
16. Superlaser power cell
17. Primary power amplifier
18. Firing field amplifier
19. Induction hyperphase generator
20. Targeting field generator
21. Primary beam focusing magnet
22. Carrier beam crystal
23. Magnetic shielding
24. Superlaser tributary beam shaft
25. Hyperdrive
26. Power cell
27. Central computer core
28. Sector computer cluster
29. Heat exchanger
30. Stellar fuel bottles
31. Cooling system
32. Refinery
33. Fuel collector

EXTERIOR
31. Quadanium steel outer hull
32. Polar trench
33. Superlaser focus lens
34. Equatorial trench
35. Mid-hemisphere trench

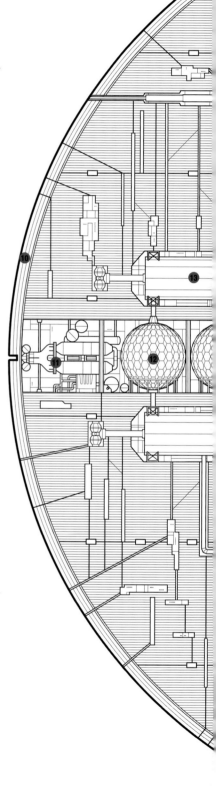

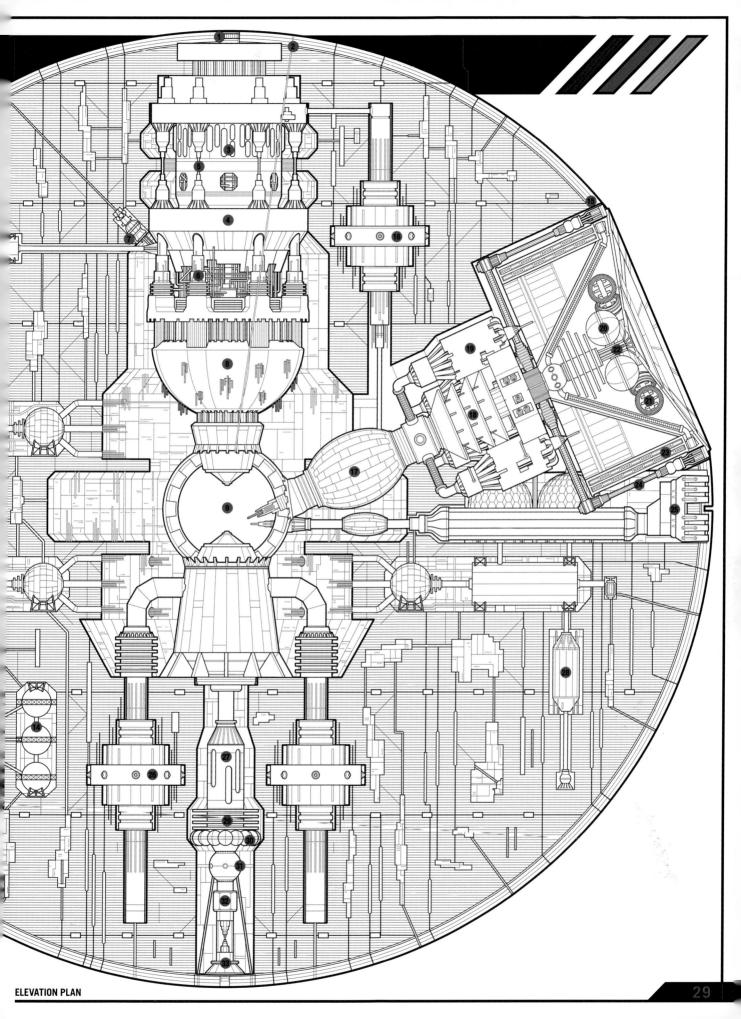

SUPERSTRUCTURE

esigned and engineered to accommodate an enormous reactor core and superlaser, the Death Star's superstructure resembled a vast network of crisscrossing girders, braces, compression-resistant struts, and interconnected tubes used for ventilation, repulsorlift travel, and the routing of energy systems. The superstructure's structural integrity was so great that the Death Star could easily withstand bombardment to its exterior or collisions with large spacecraft, and was also more resilient to external gravitational forces than smaller, non-spherical battle stations.

The voids between the superstructure's crisscrossing components were spacious enough to allow construction droids and service vehicles to travel from one area of the Death Star to another during construction. After construction was completed, repulsorlift-equipped maintenance droids moved between the components,

scanning for any sign of pressure leaks, weak welds, or other hazards that posed even a slight threat to the structure's integrity.

Despite the superstructure's strength, the first Death Star's designers did not anticipate several acts of sabotage during construction. In one instance, a bomb detonated in a cargo hold, causing significant damage to the hold and the area around it, which prompted an investigation by Darth Vader. Despite this and other acts of sabotage, and also an assault of rebel starfighters at the Battle of Yavin, the Death Star's superstructure remained sound until that battle's explosive conclusion. At the Battle of Endor, the Rebel Alliance was able to take advantage of the fact that large regions of the second Death Star's superstructure remained exposed, enabling pilots to travel straight to the station's reactor core.

⬇ From the bridge of an Imperial Star Destroyer, Emperor Palpatine and his Sith Lord lieutenant Darth Vader surveyed the construction of the Death Star.

→ The Death Star's bowels was a multilayered maze of tubes, girders, and machinery.

← Excess energy from the reactor core was diverted to lighting systems inside the superstructure, enabling construction crews to clearly see their work areas.

⬇ Although substantial voids were included for the passage of large service vehicles, such voids did not compromise structural integrity.

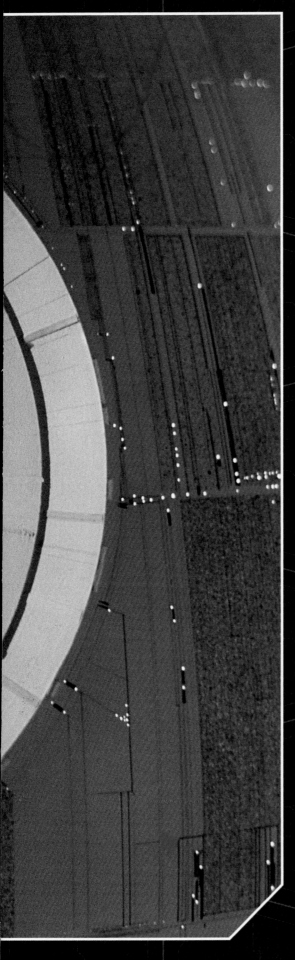

WEAPONS & DEFENSIVE SYSTEMS

Excerpts from Personal Data Journal Entries #476 and #481, Tarkin recording

The Death Star must feature a single weapon of mass destruction. This weapon must emit energy of such a degree as to rock a target planet to its very core.

In addition, the Death Star must include surface defenses rivaling that of the Imperial core worlds. Planetary shielding, surface-to-air turbolasers, 360-degree sensor capability, powerful multi-directional tractor beams, and heavy cannons for use against capital-class ships are not only necessary but vital to the design and mission of the battle station.

Chief Bevel Lemelisk assures me that he can include a weapon he calls a "superlaser" into the final design. In fact, the entire sphere will be dedicated to the support and maintenance of this single weapon. Not only will it be able to rock a planet, Bevel claims that the superlaser will shatter worlds. Only asteroid ruins will remain afer the weapon is trained upon a target.

However, to achieve such immense destructive power, I must lose all but the most rudimentary shielding capabtilities. Bevel assures me that the surface-to-air defenses will more than make up for the loss.

← Full view of the Death Star's superlaser focus lens, which was frequently referred to by Death Star gunners as "The Eye".

TRACTOR BEAM REACTOR COUPLING

Tractor beams are invisible, maneuverable force fields that can capture, shift, or redirect objects with great precision. The force field is produced by a tractor-beam generator, then released by a tractor-beam projector—also called an emitter tower—which is usually mounted on a rotating turret. Standard equipment in all spaceports and space stations, tractor beams are typically used for traffic control to guide starships into and out of hangars and docking bays.

Each zone of the Death Star featured 24 tractor-beam emplacements that housed modified Phylon Q7 tractor beam projectors—the same models used on Imperial Star Destroyers—as offensive weapons. Every zone could concentrate from one to all 24 emplacements on a single target, and at great distances, enabling the Death Star to snare distant enemy ships in a virtually unbreakable bubble of energy. The long-range projectors were so powerful that a ship could be captured before its sensors could identify the "small moon" in its vicinity as a battle station. Each Phylon Q7 tractor beam projector required a crew of ten to operate properly.

The Death Star's tractor beams were coupled to the station's main reactor to provide a steady stream of energy, which prevented accidents caused by generator malfunctions. The Death Star had seven power coupling terminals; each standing atop a generator tower 35km tall, and providing energy for more than 700 tractor beams. If the tractor beam's connection to the reactor was severed at any one of the coupling sites, the beam became inoperative. Maintenance and technician droids accessed the reactor coupling controls via a bridge that wrapped around the terminal.

→ As revealed by visual data obtained from a military communications complex on Galvoni III, Imperial stormtroopers did not detect the Jedi Knight Obi-Wan Kenobi as he shut down Tractor Beam 12 in Section N6 of the Death Star.

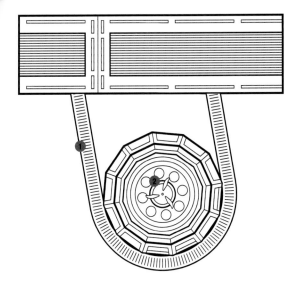

1. Maintenance bridge
2. Energy emitter
3. Control levers
4. Power level indicator
5. Status display
6. Manual override
7. Generator tower

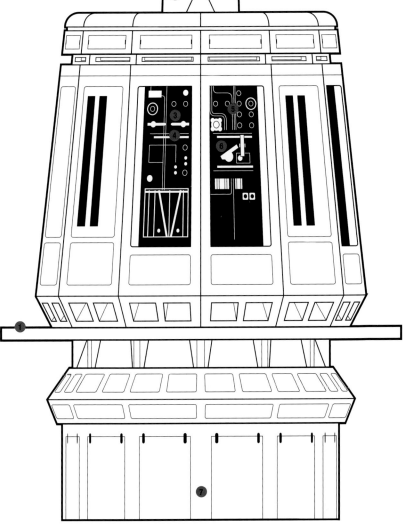

↑ The tractor beam power level indicator also displays data related to the reactor coupling's location with the Death Star.

↓ Located in the Death Star's central core, the Tractor Beam Reactor Coupling tower was approximately 35km tall.

Shield-projection towers emitted energy fields that covered the Death Star's city sprawls. These energy shields protected the sprawls from space debris, and offered limited defense against energy weapons, as most of the Death Star's energy was harnessed for operations related to the superlaser. A typical city sprawl was protected by at least three shield projection towers. Power cells, machinery, and shield-operator stations were located in the enclosed complex located at the base of each tower. The most heavily shielded area of the Death Star was the tower that accommodated the Emperor's throne room.

Shield operation fell under the jurisdiction of Battle Station Operations. Officers, operators, and technicians manned the shield-projection tower's stations to ensure the shields were always in full working order. In the event of an attack, towers from neighboring sprawls could overlap their shields to create a continuous blanket of energy over the Death Star's surface.

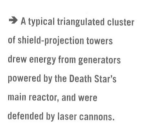

1 Shield-projection tower **3** Energizer
2 Shield generator **4** Power tap to main reactor

→ A typical triangulated cluster of shield-projection towers drew energy from generators powered by the Death Star's main reactor, and were defended by laser cannons.

ARMORED PLATING/HULL

Much of the metal for the Death Star's hull plating was drawn from asteroidal material, and processed into military-grade Quadanium steel. As if the sourcing and manufacturing of the plating were not enough of a challenge, Bevel Lemelisk's design team was also tasked with the enormous undertaking of the plating's installation.

The incredible magnitude of the project prohibited the possibility of building the space station's entire hull and pressurizing its interior before beginning interior construction, as the amount of air necessary for pressurization would have been tremendous. However, pressurized areas would be required for the estimated hundreds of thousands of laborers who would be conscripted to work on the Death Star, and those laborers would require somewhere convenient to live during the construction, as it would have been neither time nor cost effective for the Empire to shuttle laborers back and forth for any distance between shifts.

Lemelisk's team determined that the most efficient solution was to build, seal, and pressurize individual sectors while the hull was being laid. This allowed storage space for supplies during construction, and also for temporary habitats for laborers.

↑ From a distance, the Death Star's hull appeared relatively smooth to the naked eye.

↓ Heavily armored towers were constructed for turbolaser emplacements and also mooring platforms for Imperial Star Destroyers. These also served as directional markers for TIE fighter pilots.

TURBOLASER TOWER

The most common capital ship weapons in the galaxy, turbolasers are two-stage supercharged laser cannons. The small primary laser produces an energy beam that enters the turbolaser's main actuator, where it interacts with a stream of energized blaster gas to produce an intense blast. The barrel's galven coils focus the beam, providing a range that is double or triple that of conventional laser cannons. The destructive power of the fired energy bolt can punch through an enemy warship's shields and thick armor plating.

The Death Star had 5,000 Taim & Bak xx-9 heavy turbolaser towers. A typical tower featured four distinct sections housed within an armored hull. The top section housed the gun turret, which rotated in a full circle to provide a continuous arc of fire. Twin laser barrels jutted from the turret, and swivel mounts allowed the barrels to cover the vertical field of fire.

The second section of the tower contained rows of capacitor banks, which stored energy that the laser actuator converted into charged beams of intense light. This energy-storage capability was crucial to enable the turbolasers to maintain rapid fire.

The third section housed the support crew and maintenance stations, and also the substantial turbine generators required to power the tower.

The lowermost section of the tower contained the gunnery stations and the tracking and targeting computers. Although gunners wore specialized helmets that helped them provide limited targeting for their guns, only the targeting computers could keep track of multiple targets and devise fire patterns to pick out fast-moving enemy starfighters.

Safety features built into the targeting computers didn't allow the lasers to fire when any portion of the Death Star was within their sights. The Alliance exploited this vulnerability by flying their starfighters so close to the Death Star that the Imperial weapons automatically held their fire.

➡ ⬊ Turbolasers deliver a big punch but require a delay of at least two seconds between shots to allow the capacitators to build up an adequate charge.

WEAPONS & DEFENSIVE SYSTEMS

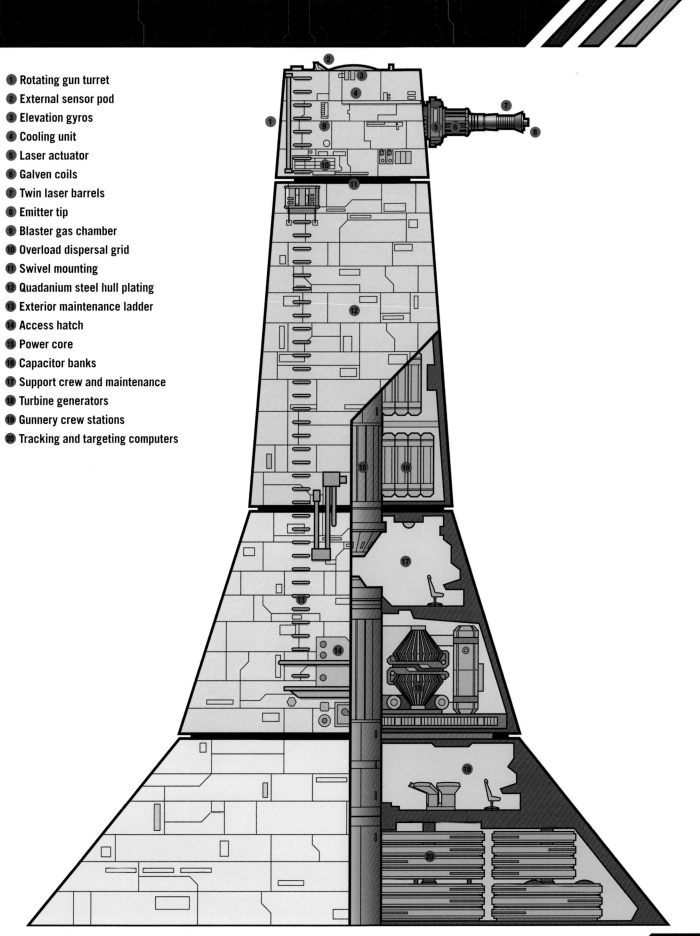

1. Rotating gun turret
2. External sensor pod
3. Elevation gyros
4. Cooling unit
5. Laser actuator
6. Galven coils
7. Twin laser barrels
8. Emitter tip
9. Blaster gas chamber
10. Overload dispersal grid
11. Swivel mounting
12. Quadanium steel hull plating
13. Exterior maintenance ladder
14. Access hatch
15. Power core
16. Capacitor banks
17. Support crew and maintenance
18. Turbine generators
19. Gunnery crew stations
20. Tracking and targeting computers

Defenses along the Death Star's trenches included Borstel Galactic Defense Super Blaster 920 laser cannons, exotic energy weapons manufactured exclusively for Imperial starships. The SB-920 is capable of destroying shields and armor on capital ships, and can destroy a starfighter with a single shot.

Like most laser cannons, the SB-920 funnels volatile blaster gas from a supercooled and armored chamber, combines the gas with a power charge, and directs the resulting energy through a long barrel. Circuitry in the barrel increases the beam's power. Where the SB-920 differs substantially from other laser cannons is that instead of relying on a built-in computerized targeting system to help a single gunner track targets, the cannon is linked to tactical computer systems throughout the Death Star, and requires a crew of three: a standing gunner, a seated targeting technician, and a seated energy technician. The SB-920 also has a faster recharge rate than most laser cannons.

Each member of the SB-920 crew wears protective, specialized computer helmets equipped with arrays to assist with their respective duties. The targeting technician monitors and analyzes the targeting computer systems to help the gunner select the best target, be it a fast-moving fighter craft or a specific shield generator on a capital ship. The energy technician ensures the cannon doesn't overheat or run out of power. The gunner selects targets, maneuvers the cannon, and operates the trigger.

The SB-920 utilizes an advanced Target Acquisition and Tracking (TAT) system similar to certain Imperial surface-to-air defensive systems. The TAT acquires a signature lock on targets in a designated vector while the computer selects a primary target, and simultaneously updates and calculates trajectories of alternate targets. The TAT extrapolates the position of receding targets at long range, and the SB-920 crew is quite capable of bringing those targets down.

At the Battle of Yavin, Death Star gunners prevented most of the rebel starfighters from reaching the battle station's exhaust port canyon. However, data recovered from an Imperial communications complex on Galvoni III revealed that shortly before the Battle of Yavin, an overzealous officer under General Tagge, in a misguided attempt to encourage Death Star gunner crews to become effective in any combination, redistributed the gunners in alphabetical order throughout the battle station. By that one order, the close-knit unity of the gun crews and their targeting coordinators may have been swept away, and aided the rebel victory at Yavin.

→ Death Star gunners are stationed in pressurized enclosures to fire the cannons directly through magnetic force-field ports. Gunners wear specialized computer helmets equipped with arrays to assist with targeting fast-moving fighter craft.

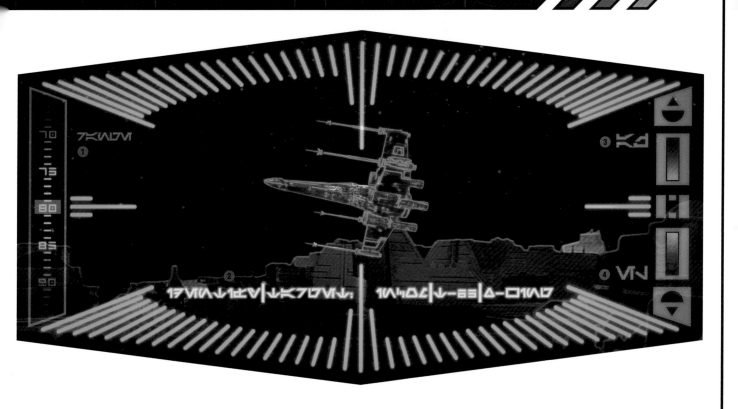

↑ An example of a Target Acquisition and Tracking (TAT) system technical readout, displayed within an SB-920 gunner's computer helmet, presents an attack simulation of an enemy X-wing starfighter above a Death Star trench.

1 Range indicator
2 Target identifier
3 Azimuth (degree of rotation)
4 Elevation (vertical angle)

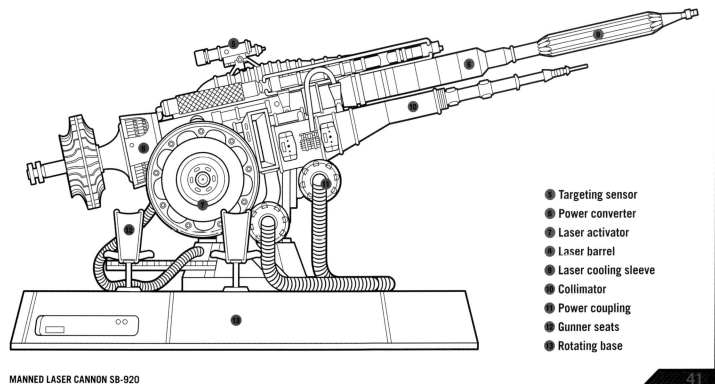

5 Targeting sensor
6 Power converter
7 Laser activator
8 Laser barrel
9 Laser cooling sleeve
10 Collimator
11 Power coupling
12 Gunner seats
13 Rotating base

SUPERLASER

The majority of the Death Star's interior volume was dedicated to housing and supporting its primary weapon: the superlaser keystone to Emperor Palpatine's "Doctrine of Fear". The weapon's energy originated deep within the battle station, and was channeled into an array of eight initiator laser cannons. The tributary beams from the eight cannons converged at a central amplification nexus over the superlaser cannon well—the vast concavity in the Death Star's upper hemisphere—to form a powerful single beam. The power of this beam could be controlled and scaled to suit the destruction of various targets. A beam of one power level could be used against enemy capital ships. The most powerful beam had more firepower than half the Imperial Starfleet, and could instantly reduce a world to asteroid fragments and space dust.

At an early stage of the Death Star's development, the challenges of building an operational superlaser led to a proposal for an alternative weapon: a composite beam superlaser. This weapon would have fired proton beams capable of destroying a planet's core, and leaving the targeted planet uninhabitable. The composite beam superlaser would have required an immense mechanical arm to move the superlaser's concave dish out of a locked position—flush with the battle station's spherical surface—before firing. However, engineers were able to resolve the technical difficulties of the planet-shattering superlaser, and plans for the composite beam superlaser were scrapped.

The superlaser's power required recharging between firings, and the intensity of each firing determined the per-day firing frequency, from once per minute against spaceborne vessels to once every 24 hours against planetary targets. Recovered Imperial reports indicate the superlaser, prior to destroying Alderaan, also destroyed the *Fortressa*, a *Lucrehulk*-class battleship under rebel control, and the prison planet Despayre.

↓ Front view of the Superlaser. The cannon well's diameter was approximately 35km.

1. **Primary power amplifer**
2. **Inulator plating**
3. **Induction hyperphase generator**
4. **Firing field amplifer**
5. **Superlaser tributary beam shaft**
6. **Magnetic shielding**
7. **Primary beam focusing magnet**
8. **Targeting field generator**
9. **Carrier beam crystal**

DEATH STAR GUNNERS

A special sub-unit of the Imperial pilot corp, Death Star gunners were culled from the best fighting units in the galaxy. Many were originally Imperial Navy pilots-in-training or pilots who failed to qualify for flight assignment, who nonetheless possessed keen eyes, superior reflexes, and a rapport with specialized equipment. Gunners were expected to be able to handle everything from a single light laser cannon to turbolaser battery emplacements.

Death Star gunners were trained to work as a group, to operate gun towers and defend against large-scale assault, and specialized in unified fire and probability-generated spread patterns. In the event of attack from enemy starfighters, gunners would operate cannons from multiple emplacements to blanket the Death Star in a defensive net of blaster fire. The Death Star's highest-ranking and best-trained gunners were assigned to the superlaser.

The gunners wore specialized computer helmets that not only offered protection but were equipped with macrobinocular viewplates, sensor arrays to assist with targeting fast-moving fighter craft, and sophisticated tracking systems for better fire control assistance. Each helmet was also equipped with a tongue-operated comlink.

Prior to the Battle of Yavin, Death Star gunners spent months calibrating their weapons, running through countless scenario engagements. Utilizing battle plans devised by Tarkin's staff, a thousand simulated rebel fleets engaged the Death Star, and a thousand rebel fleets were repelled and destroyed. Evidently, it never occurred to the Imperials that they should test themselves against a simulated attack by small squadrons of starfighters instead of just a large armada.

⬇ Computer-linked helmets and thousands of hours of drilling enabled Death Star gunners to aim, power-up, and fire the superlaser with synchronized precision.

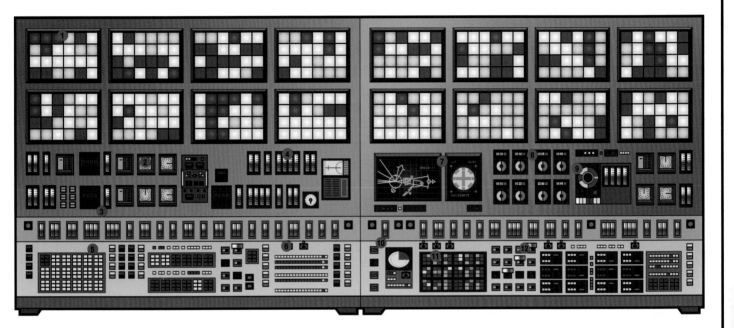

1. System status boards
2. Energy transfer relays
3. Radiation levels
4. Emitter crystal harmonics
5. Laser station sychronization
6. Targeting sensor refinement
7. Targeting displays
8. Tributary beam alignment
9. Focus-field polarity
10. Charge status-indicator
11. System ignition keypad
12. System ignition keypad

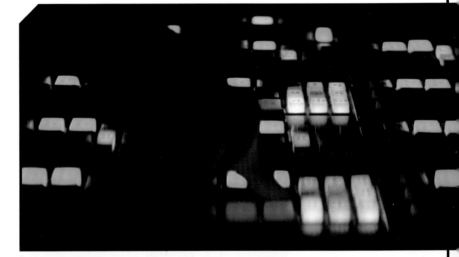

Eight individually manned laser stations produced the beams of super-charged energy for the Death Star's superlaser. In case one of the main laser stations malfunctioned, four back-up laser stations were always on active standby.

The eight beams of energy converged at a central amplification nexus in front of the huge, concave focus lens. For optimum performance, the superlaser was manned by 168 Imperial gunners, with a minimum of 14 soldiers manning each of the initiator laser cannons.

SUPERLASER TRIBUTARY BEAM SHAFT

Of all the Death Star's technological challenges, the greatest was engineering the superlaser, and all its numerous safeguards, to prevent the battle station from being destroyed by its own incredible power. Some of these challenges had already been addressed and resolved by Project Hammertong, a top-secret weapon project that originated during the Clone Wars.

Authorized by then-Supreme Chancellor Palpatine, Hammertong was developed to explore the use of laser-stream technology for a new weapon. Hammertong incorporated crystal technology that Republic forces seized from an experimental power source on the planet Mygeeto, where the native Muun had long drawn power from synthesized crystals, and built their cities around enormous capacitor towers that stored and distributed energy. Hammertong's laser-stream weapon required tributary beam shafts, which—after the foundation of the Empire—were constructed at

Desolation Station, an Imperial facility in the Atrivis sector. Evidently, the Death Star project superseded Hammertong, for the beam shafts were subsequently transported to the Death Star's construction site.

Eight tributary beam shafts, each with its own amplification crystal, were positioned around the circumference of the superlaser's immense concave cannon well. The shafts were lined with focusing coils to maintain each beam's integrity. The tributary beams had to be perfectly calibrated and aligned, or the central beam would misfocus and dissipate, and generate a flurry of backscatter that could severely damage or destroy the superlaser housing. The firing process also generated magnetic fields and gravitational flux, which had to be dissipated to prevent the amplification crystals from becoming misaligned, and to prevent the battle station from being torn apart.

→ Although the visors on Death Star gunner helmets were designed to protect the gunners' eyes, visual data obtained from an Imperial communications complex reveal some gunners in the tributary beam shaft routinely left their lower faces partially exposed, presumably to maintain direct audio communication with fellow gunners when the shaft was filled by static charges from the tributary beam.

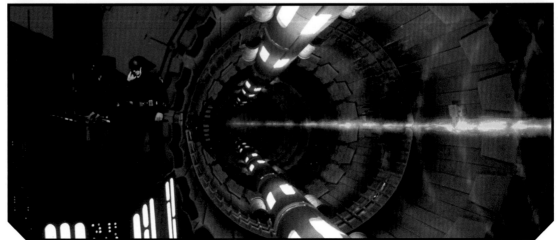

1. **Principle energy inducer**
2. **Primary focusing coils**
3. **Gravitational flux dampeners**
4. **Amplification crystal chamber**
5. **Galven coils**
6. **Collimator**
7. **Pulse capacitor**
8. **Magnetic dissipators**
9. **Fine targeting coils**

↑ The locations of the Death Star's tributary beam shafts are illustrated on page 43.

← Despite the gunners' protective visors, control stations in the tributary shaft were positioned so the gunners would stand with their backs to the beam, preventing them from glancing at the brilliant stream of energy directly. Gunners closed their eyes before the beam blazed at full intensity.

ENERGY & PROPULSION

Excerpts from Personal Data Journal Entries #461 and 481, Grand Moff Tarkin recording

Because the Death Star's energy requirements are as staggering as the challenges of building a weapon that can actually contain and release such energy without destroying itself, it's easy to understand why Raith Sienar essentially abandoned his concepts for the Expeditionary Battle Planetoid. To generate and control such energy, the battle station must be enormous. Much of its interior will consist of housing for the giant power cells, engines, weapons systems, and other machinery necessary to support living beings and actually move the sphere through space.

The Death Star not only needs to move through normal space but it must also have the capacity to travel through hyperspace or it is useless to us. While hyperspace speeds need not be great, since a planet would not be able to evade this station, it would be pleasing to achieve a moderate hyperdrive multiplier.

Moving the sphere will be accomplished through the use of massive ion sublight drives while in realspace, and through redundant hyperdrive engines for travel from system to system. Make no mistake, though. The Death Star will be slow. It will seem to crawl through the void between planets, and even in hyperspace it will be no faster than the most ancient tramp freighter. [Engineer] Bevel [Lemelisk] believes that he can get the hyperdrive multiplier down to three, but he warns me that it could be as high as five or six. No matter. It is fitting that targets of this station have an exceptionally long period of time to fear their ultimate fate.

HYPERMATTER REACTOR

→ Holographic schematics revealed the second Death Star held a more sophisticated hypermatter reactor than its predecessor.

The Death Star's primary power generator was a cavernous SFS-CR27200 hypermatter reactor, a chamber lined by stellar fuel bottles that fed a fusion reaction of prodigious proportions. This reactor powered all systems on the battle station, including the superlaser and turbolaser emplacements, 123 Isu-Sim SSP06 hyperdrive generators and two Sepma 30-5 sublight engines, energy shields, and life-support.

The hypermatter reactor was located at the center of the Death Star's cylindrical polar column, which served to distribute power and stabilize the station's rotational capabilities. Capacitor panels were layered around the reactor core, and reactor shafts extended outward to the station's circumference.

↓→ Although visual recordings of the first Death Star's hypermatter reactor may be lost to time, the Rebel Allliance obtained close-up views of the second Death Star's power transference assembly, and images of the considerably larger reactor.

The Death Star was engineered with innumerable redundant engine and electrical subsystems to ensure power could be directed to any area of the battle station when necessary. Not only were all of the Death Star's subsystems interconnected but they were also connected to the main reactor system in order to provide maximum power to all subsystems at all times.

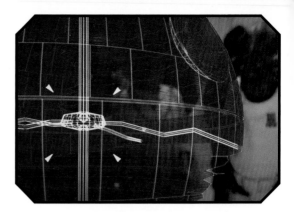

FIRST DEATH STAR'S HYPERMATTER REACTOR

1. Lines out to power distribution nodes
2. Main power generator
3. Static discharge vanes
4. Clean/filtered power manifolds
5. Energy exchanger
6. Raw power manifolds
7. Radiation insulator plating
8. Containment field coils
9. Reaction chamber
10. Superlaser power diverters
11. Raw power to superlaser
12. Hyperdrive power diverter
13. Raw power to hyperdrive
14. Fuel injectors
15. Power diverter manifold control
16. Primary fuel exciters
17. Fuel control valves
18. Raw fuel supply lines (from stellar fuel bottles)
19. Power regulators
20. Emergency raw power diversion solonoid
21. Line out to power cell

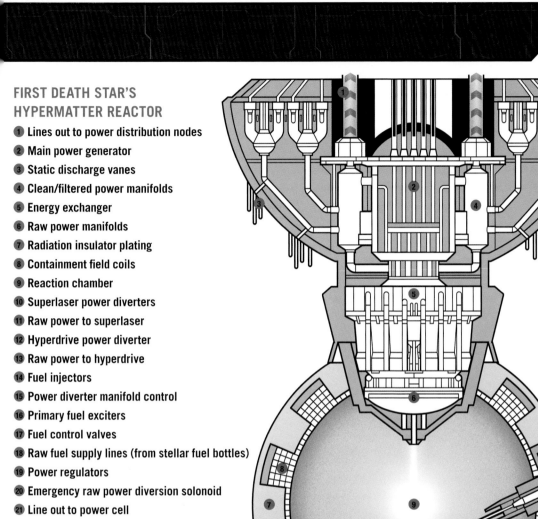
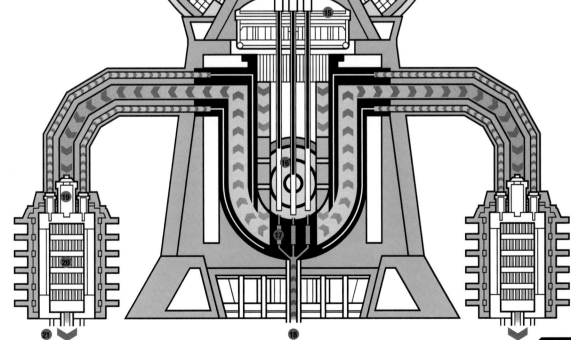

THERMAL EXHAUST PORT

Excess energy produced by the Death Star's hypermatter reactor was expelled into space by way of thermal exhaust ports, which were scattered over the battle station's surface. Although the exhaust ports effectively prevented excess heat and radiation from damaging the station or injuring crew members, they were especially vulnerable to attack, as they opened upon shafts that lead directly to the reactor. The Death Star's designers, knowing that an explosion within an exhaust port could trigger a chain reaction that might damage or destroy the main reactor, utilized ray-shield generators to protect the exhaust ports from laser bombardment.

After obtaining the Death Star's technical readouts, the Rebel Alliance determined protective ray shields could be breached by projectiles such as proton torpedoes. The Alliance concluded that a precise hit on one exhaust port's shaft would ignite an explosion that would start a series of energy backlashes that would travel from subsystem to subsystem, and explode in proximity to the main reactor. Alliance tacticians surmised that if the Death Star's designers had not engineered the station with so many interconnected systems, a single proton torpedo might have partially crippled the battle station but would not have destroyed it.

⬇ **Technical readouts revealed that an innocuous, two-meter-wide thermal exhaust port was the Death Star's most vulnerable area.**

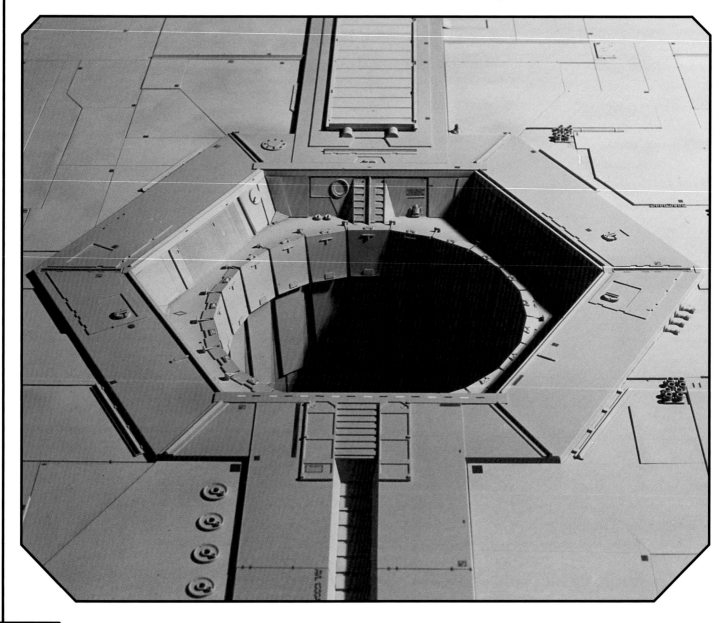

Inside the rebel base on Yavin 4, a viewscreen displayed the Death Star's technical readouts while General Jan Dodonna briefed pilots and astromech droids on his strategy to attack the battle station. Dodonna instructed the pilots to fire proton torpedoes into a specific thermal exhaust port.

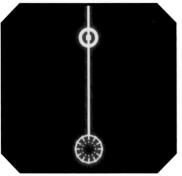

⬆ Strategic animatic of a proton torpedo traveling into the shaft beneath the exhaust port.

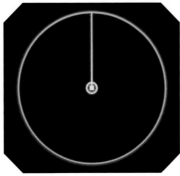

⬆ The ray-shielded exhaust port's shaft led directly to the Death Star's reactor system.

⬆ A precise hit would trigger a chain reaction that would destroy the entire battle station.

← Rebel starfighters swarmed the Death Star in a coordinated effort to reach their target.

Although hyperdrives are considered much 'cleaner' than their highly-radioactive sublight drive counterparts, they require more power to hurl their host beyond lightspeed. The Death Star's hyperspace motivator units comprised linked banks of field generators—the same systems used by Imperial Star Destroyers. One hundred twenty-three individual hyperspace generators, tied into a single navigational matrix, were necessary to carry the Death Star beyond the speed of light. The intense power generated within the battle station, combined with its great mass, gave it both magnetic and artificial gravitational fields equal to those of a natural body many times its size.

Every hyperdrive station on the Death Star had dedicated astrogation/hyperdrive computers. Collectively, these computers housed coordinates for every system in Imperial Space, and also thousands of other systems that the Empire intended to conquer. As with any hyperdrive-equipped vessel, all hyperspace jump calculations had to be incredibly precise to guarantee that the Death Star would arrive completely intact at any given destination. Engineers and technicians manned the hyperdrive stations' control stations, checking and cross-checking their linked computer monitors to make certain that all of the Death Star's hyperdrives worked in unison.

Retractable footbridges extended between the hyperdrive stations' control stations and the central power core, allowing engineers and technicians to inspect the power core's energy readouts, check for stresses or leaks, and make any necessary repairs. Because of high radiation levels, Imperial personnel relied on droids to inspect the power core while the Death Star was traveling through hyperspace.

⬇ From the Overbridge, Darth Vader and Grand Moff Tarkin monitored the battle station's hyperspace jump to Alderaan. Moving such a large mass through hyperspace required the coordinated effort of all hyperdrive stations.

← A view of the planet Alderaan from the Death Star, shortly before Alderaan's destruction. The Death Star's hyperdrive system was linked with the navicomputer to deliver the battle station to strategic areas beyond the hazardous range of planetary or stellar gravitational forces.

1. Charge coils
2. Effect channels
3. Energy junction
4. Field stabilizer plating
5. Horizontal boosters
6. Power regulator
7. Regulator access platform
8. Control station
9. Retractable footbridge
10. Turbolift
11. Open vertical shaft
12. Astrogation/hyperdrive computers

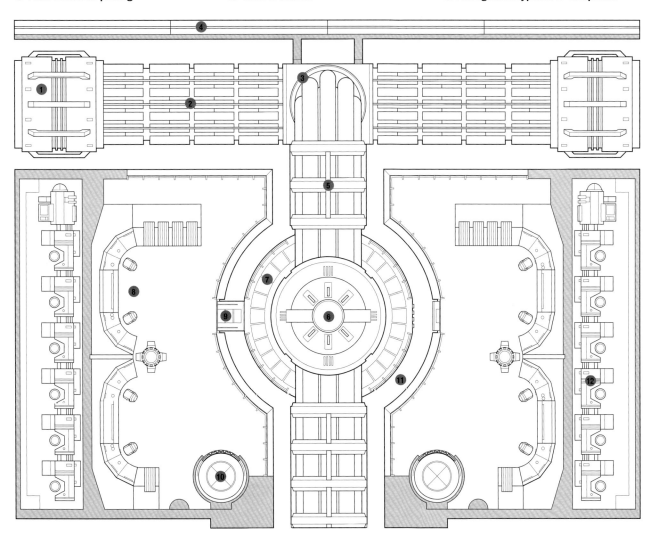

ION SUBLIGHT ENGINES

➔ After exiting hyperspace in the Yavin system, the Death Star used sublight engines to enter orbit around the giant gas planet Yavin.

The Death Star's realspace propulsion was handled by an external array of powerful ion engines, which converted the raw fusion energy of the station's core into fusion reaction particles. The converted energy was used to achieve thrust, and pressed the station's great mass into any motion dictated by the *Death Star*'s huge navicomputer banks. Engine blocks were located along the battle station's equator and also at its poles,

providing the thrust to move the massive vessel through space. While ion engines of such magnitude are highly radioactive, no other system could provide the directional control necessary for a station of such great size. Powerful vents were utilized to force the radiation out of the drive stations and into space. Engineering personnel assigned to monitor ion vent operations routinely wore protective gear to ward off radiation spillage.

1. Thrust beam
2. Focusing field stabilizer
3. Exhaust pre-stabilizer screen
4. Thrust pressure manifold
5. Ion accelator
6. Sychronizing interconnectors
7. Magnetic chamber
8. Magnetic field stabilizer
9. Initiating coils
10. Support framework
11. Electron injectors
12. Power line from reactor
13. Drive station

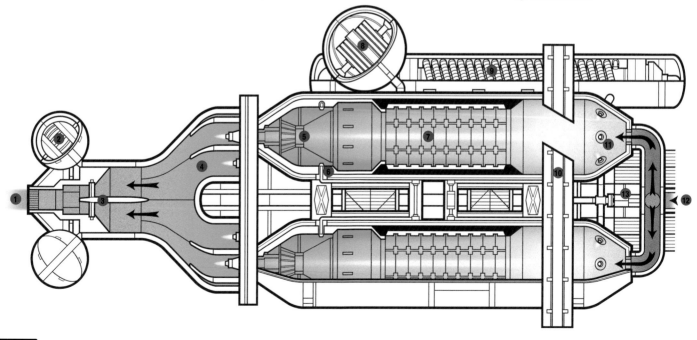

SUBLIGHT DRIVE STATION D-639

Engineering had the sole assignment of keeping the Death Star's sublight and hyperdrive engines in working order. Sublight Drive Station D-639 was a typical layout, designed for engineers and technicians to operate and monitor the sublight drives. Two main consoles overlooked a crew pit, where personnel were tasked with ensuring the sublight drives remained fully operational at all times. Although the numerous controls and equipment in the sublight drive station were constructed with durable materials, Imperial designers anticipated that the constant use of various controls would inevitably lead to some becoming damaged. The station's small parts shop enabled the engineering team to make minor repairs quickly and without leaving the station. Droid technicians were also on standby to repair or upgrade delicate circuitry.

1. Radiation vents
2. Sublight drive units
3. Power cells
4. Power level monitoring
5. Crew pit
6. Main consoles
7. Briefing room
8. Computer room
9. Turbolift cluster
10. Small parts shop
11. Engineer office
12. Auxiliary helm

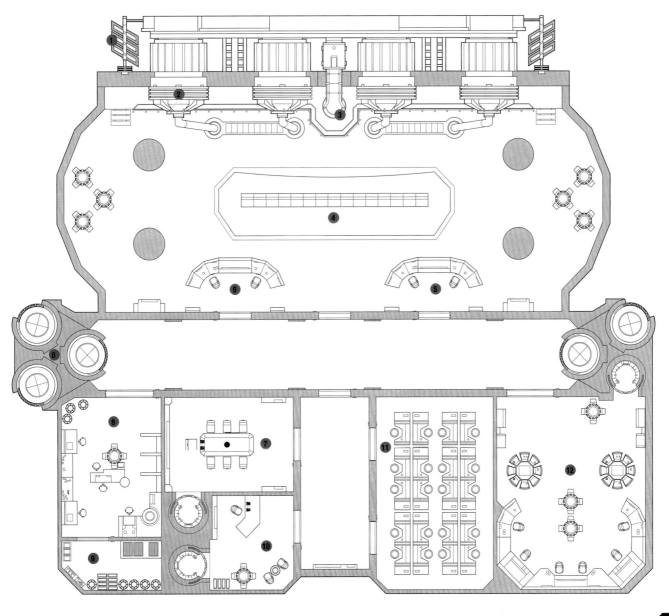

HANGAR BAYS

Excerpts from Personal Data Journal Entry
#463, Grand Moff Tarkin recording

In his initial concept designs for the Expeditionary Battle Planetoid, Raith Sienar was so preoccupied by the energy and space requirements for the massive weapon systems that he neglected to consider accommodations for the spacecraft necessary for the battle station's defense, maintenance, and other purposes. To his credit, his concepts did incorporate docking systems for large warships, and also a sophisticated network of multidirectional lift tubes, but as the design process progressed toward the construction of a much larger battle station, it became apparent that small shuttles would be more often the most efficient means of travel from one surface sector to another. Obviously, such travel would only be workable if the station had an abundance of hangars and docking bays. Furthermore, the Emperor agreed that the superweapon should be as autonomous as possible, that it would more effectively induce fear as a singular weapon of destruction than if it moved across the galaxy with a conspicuous armada.

Not surprisingly, Bevel Lemelisk's designs for the hangars have exceeded my expectations. The Death Star will easily accommodate thousands of TIE fighters, and will boast more hangar bays than the average commercial spaceport. He has strategically positioned numerous tractor beam projectors and docking bays for the express purpose of capturing enemy spacecraft.

A subtle yet most impressive accomplishment in Lemelisk's design addresses how the Death Star's many hangars and bays will be oriented with the station's expansive gravity systems. Although the majority of the Death Star's inhabited areas will be engineered for a gravity orientation that is toward the core, most of the hangar bays and the corridors that immediately surround the hangars will be built perpendicular to the core. In other words, nearly every hangar above and below the equator, as well as those along the equator itself, is engineered so gravity seems to generate from the same direction, so from almost any given hangar, the station's south pole is perceived as "down" and the north pole as "up". This orientation will not only allow ships to arrive and depart from the station in remarkably uniform trajectories, but will simplify many junctures of the lift tube systems and encourage an innate awareness to hierarchy throughout the station.

I admit, I had assumed Lemelisk would follow Sienar's original plan to place hangars at various angles along the station's surface area, but Lemelisk's solution is more than brilliant. It embraces the greatness of Imperial technology and defies the natural laws of gravity. Simply put, the Death Star is perfection.

Numerous and various-sized hangar bays ringed the Death Star like latitude lines. The larger bays were surrounded by support decks which contained vehicle maintenance shops, emergency medical stations, pilot ready rooms, and repulsorlift shafts connecting to deep storage bays. Smaller shuttle hangars could handle one or two craft and were found all over the battle station. They were normally used for station personnel movement. Ships first arriving at the Death Star or leaving for deep space normally worked with a latitude bay control tower.

Like most Death Star hangars, Docking Bay 327 had tractor beam projectors and interior emergency repulsor fields to deal with damaged vessels. Tractor beams guided craft that had lost engines or directional thrusters, and emergency generators could flood a bay with a repulsorfield cushion landings. The walls and decks were lined with power cell chargers sockets where parked craft could obtain fuel for their next mission. Directional markings etched into the deck were

illuminated by the tower to guide ships to a safe resting place. The deck was also equipped with a large lift that transported troops, vehicles, cargo, and maintenance equipment to and from the barracks, workshops, and supply rooms located below the hangar.

DEEP STORAGE DOCKING BAYS

The Death Star's innermost hangar bays held the complement of land vehicles, backup shuttles and starfighters, and special-service vessels that were not expected to be used routinely. These vehicles were contained within stasis fields that protected them from dust and vermin, keeping each craft in perfect condition. When a ship was requisitioned from a deep storage bay, repulsor-generated antigrav fields were projected into the bay, and moved the ship out of stasis and into a repulsor shaft. From the repulsor shaft, the ship could be transported to a latitude surface hangar anywhere within the battle station.

The stasis fields were checked regularly to maintain

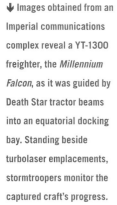

⬇ Images obtained from an Imperial communications complex reveal a YT-1300 freighter, the *Millennium Falcon*, as it was guided by Death Star tractor beams into an equatorial docking bay. Standing beside turbolaser emplacements, stormtroopers monitor the captured craft's progress.

their integrity. Security guarded the deep storage docking bays with the same dedication as personnel who oversaw the Death Star's armories.

↑ View of Hangar Bay 327 from the docking bay control room window.

↓ A large lift delivers additional stormtroopers to the docking bay.

DOCKING BAY CONTROL ROOM

Every hangar and docking bay on the Death Star had a control room, sometimes called control towers, that overlooked the hangar. Each control room was staffed by a team that monitored the approach and departure of all craft into and out of the hangars. Control teams reported to and received orders from their zone's main control tower, which was commanded by a complete staff of maintenance

→ Imperial records confirmed the identity of Lieutenant Pol Treidum, gantry officer in charge of Docking Bay 327. Treidum surveyed the docking bay from his control room window.

personnel, emergency medical teams, and flight support personnel and droids. Each zone's main control tower contained sensor relays, flight-tracking screens, ship-to-ship communication capabilities, tractor beam and repulsorlift controls, and consoles for regulating the magnetic fields in each of the hangars and docking bays within the respective zone.

A typical docking bay control room housed computer consoles that could be used to access data and monitor other areas of the Death Star. A rack of blaster rifles was positioned close to the room's doorway so the crew would have quick access to weapons in the event that an enemy infiltrated the hangar. The room also held various security supplies, including binders to secure prisoners during their escort to the detention levels.

Each zone of the Death Star had a main control tower, which contained sensor relays, flight tracking

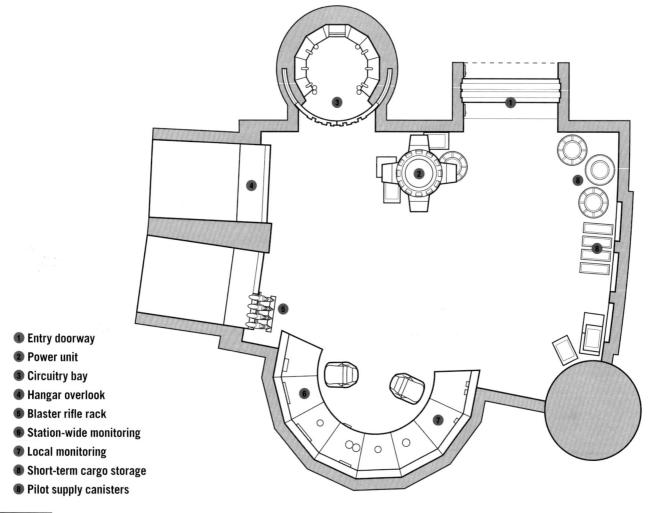

1 **Entry doorway**

2 **Power unit**

3 **Circuitry bay**

4 **Hangar overlook**

5 **Blaster rifle rack**

6 **Station-wide monitoring**

7 **Local monitoring**

8 **Short-term cargo storage**

8 **Pilot supply canisters**

screens, ship-to-ship communication capabilities, tractor beam and repulsorlift controls, and consoles for regulating the magnetic fields in each of the hangars and docking bays within the respective zone. The tower was commanded by a complete staff of maintenance personnel, emergency medical teams, and flight support personnel and droids.

↑ Docking bay control room officers monitored consoles with built-in comlinks, allowing them to communicate with Imperial stormtroopers and other personnel stationed aboard the Death Star.

↑ On the control room's consoles, monitors typically displayed data regarding vehicles, personnel, and general status inside the adjoining hangar, but could also display schematics for almost every area of the Death Star.

← After arriving on the Death Star with the crew of the *Millennium Falcon*, the droids C-3PO and R2-D2 accessed data from the docking bay control room's computer to help their allies liberate the captive Princess Leia Organa and escape the battle station.

EXECUTIVE DOCKING BAY

→ Darth Vader arrived in an executive docking bay on the second Death Star, and was met by Moff Jerjerrod, the Imperial officer who had been assigned to overseeing the battle station's construction.

Reserved for high-ranking Imperial officers and visiting dignitaries, the Death Star's executive docking bays were located within the battle station's equatorial trench, and were extremely expansive. These bays were more heavily reinforced than those used by typical Imperial transports and starships, with additional energy-shield generators, tractor-beam projectors, and laser cannons emplaced in and around the trench walls to ensure trouble-free arrivals and departures. Small droids equipped with micro-cleaning systems were tasked with keeping all surface areas within the bays spotless and free of dust.

The largest executive docking bay was constructed specifically for Emperor Palpatine, and could accommodate hundreds of troops for arrival ceremonies. A smaller executive docking bay, reserved for Darth Vader, was located near the Emperor's bay. Both bays were designed to receive and deploy *Lambda*-class shuttles.

Like other Death Star docking bays, the executive bays had openings that appeared to be exposed to the vacuum of space. The openings were protected by powerful magnetic fields that maintained the atmosphere within the bays, but the fields could be manipulated in intensity to allow starships to enter and exit the bays. If bay control crews anticipated the arrival of a vessel with shield or engine damage,

↓ During the Death Star's construction, scores of Imperial stormtroopers stood in formation as the Emperor arrived to inspect the battle station.

they could empty the bay of all personnel except for those in protective gear, and close the bay's blast doors to form vacuum-worthy seals to retain station atmosphere integrity.

→ One of the Death Star's docking bay's was reserved for Darth Vader's *Lambda*-class T-4a shuttle, manufactured by Cygnus Spaceworks.

→ From the moment that an executive vessel's ramp was lowered, all personnel within the docking bay were required by Imperial regulations to stand at attention.

→ Flanked by a receiving party, a senior officer was prepared to immediately debrief Darth Vader about the Death Star's status.

TIE HANGAR

While many of the Death Star's hangar bays were equipped to accommodate shuttles and other transports, most were engineered specifically to house, deploy, and service Imperial TIE fighters, which are not equipped with landing gear. The Death Star carried more than 7,000 TIE fighters. Smaller hangars contained as few as two TIE fighters, while larger hangars contained six squadrons, or 72 TIE fighters.

Each TIE hangar bay had ceiling-mounted racks that held the TIEs several meters above the deck. Pilots climbed across a gantry above the racks to reach their starfighters, and entered the TIEs through ceiling hatches. After the pilot was seated behind the controls and the hatch was sealed, the rack disengaged and dropped the TIE into the waiting repulsorlift field below. The field maneuvered the TIE to the bay opening where tractor beams automatically took control, catapulting the TIE through the hangar's magnetic forcefield and into space. When the TIE returned to the hangar, tractor beams would guide the TIE back onto the rack.

Surrounding decks were designed to offer total support to the starfighters and their pilots. The Death Star's largest TIE bays accommodated two full wings of TIEs, dwarfing similar TIE-exclusive bays in most Star Destroyers, which only held half of a wing.

① **Ship gantry**
② **Pilot catwalk**
③ **Boarding platform**
④ **Ladder**
⑤ **Ingress/egress hatch**
⑥ **Cockpit viewport**
⑦ **Retaining claw**
⑧ **Launch release guide**
⑨ **Solar array wing**
⑩ **Wing brace**
⑪ **Laser cannon**

⬇ An elite corps within the Imperial Navy, Imperial pilots undergo a strenuous screening and testing process for admission into the TIE training program. The Death Star had 167,216 pilots.

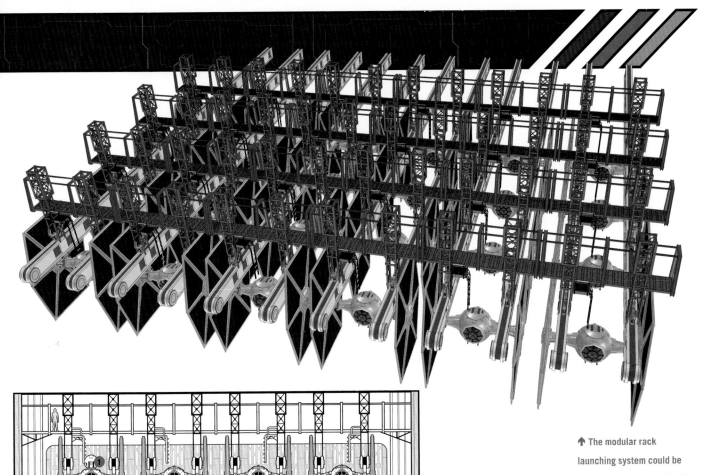

1. Open hatch
2. Transfer tunnel
3. Access doors
4. Refueling pod
5. Open blast doors
6. Service gantry

⬆ The modular rack launching system could be adjusted to accommodate the maximum capacity of TIEs in different sized hangars.

⬇ A TIE bomber, secured above a hangar bay floor, carried a payload that included orbital mines and proton bombs.

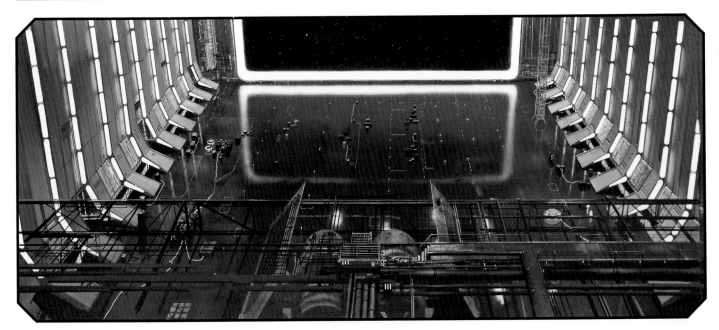

CITY SPRAWLS & TRENCHES

Excerpt from the Personal Diary of Imperial Admiral Conan Antonio Motti, commander of the Naval operations aboard the Death Star.

From a distance, the Death Star resembles an airless, runaway moon with a large, single impact crater. But upon closer inspection, it becomes apparent that this 'moon' is hardly a natural body. The crater has an obvious symmetry that could never be the result of some random impact. Below the crater, a dark line wraps around the sphere's equator, bisecting its upper and lower hemispheres. Canyons, ridges, and valleys come into view, but unlike natural formations these surface details run in parallel lines and at right angles, and form true geometric patterns.

The 'crater', of course, is what Death Star gunners call the 'Eye', the collector lens that focuses the superlaser. The dark line at the equator is a trench that holds docking bays and weapons emplacements, and this trench is linked to many others. And all the formations on the surface are actually expanses of modular Imperial constructions that form city sprawls. Although the superlaser is certainly the battle station's most prominent feature, the trenches and sprawls are no less amazing. All those interconnected clusters and masses of thermal exhaust ports, heat sinks, sublight thrusters, hyperdrive thrusters, transparisteel viewports, cosmic-ray sinks, energy flush vents, and navigation lights add up to the most awe-inspiring invention, the most incredible weapon.

I wish I could see the faces of the Empire's enemies when they first behold the Death Star, and they immediately realize that they are powerless to defend themselves. I want very much to personally witness the fear in their eyes.

⇐ This image, recorded by a damaged astromech droid from the aft of a rebel-piloted X-wing starfighter, shows a TIE fighter and a TIE Advanced x1 prototype fighter in the Death Star's latitudinal polar trench during the Battle of Yavin.

CITY SPRAWL NORTH 7: A68

Because prefabricated Imperial building materials were used for most of the Death Star's habitable sections, structures and layouts of the city sprawls strongly resembled planetary Imperial outposts and research stations. City Sprawl North 7: A68, located in the Death Star's northern hemisphere, zone N7, was typical of the hundreds of regional constructs that dotted the battle station's surface. Turbolasers were housed on multi-storied towers that were grouped into skyline batteries, all strategically positioned to work together in combined offensive attacks. Huge workstations supported and operated shield projectors alongside space-traffic control towers. Giant communications islands, bordered by myriad sensor arrays, handled outgoing and incoming holo and voice transmissions.

Although City Sprawl North 7: A68 operated as an independent 'village', its sensors and communications nets constantly fed data to Zone N7's command sector computers, which in turn fed to the overbridge interior

central computers for analysis and compilation. The computers collectively created a complete view of all activity and the overall status of the Death Star's exterior for the command sector's perusal. When more coordinated activity was necessary to examine, repair, or defend city sprawls, the overbridge could take control of the computers in every zone.

City Sprawl North 7: A68 had representatives from all the major sectors operating aboard the Death Star. Command, military, security, service/technical, hangar, and general sectors maintained operation centers within the confines of the sprawl. Each operation center had a commanding officer who reported to interior command. The chain of command worked up to Operations Command and the command triumvirate of Grand Moff Tarkin, Admiral Motti, and General Tagge.

⬇ Zone N7 of the Death Star's northern hemisphere.

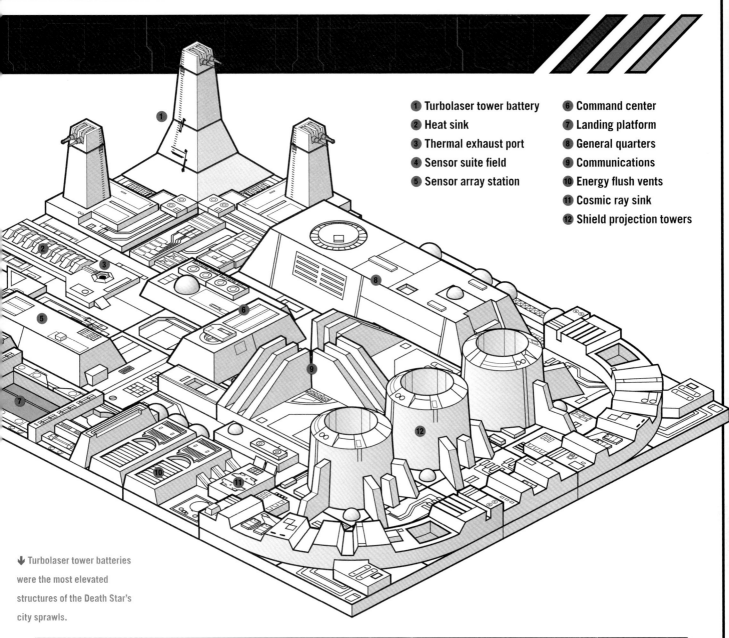

1. Turbolaser tower battery
2. Heat sink
3. Thermal exhaust port
4. Sensor suite field
5. Sensor array station
6. Command center
7. Landing platform
8. General quarters
9. Communications
10. Energy flush vents
11. Cosmic ray sink
12. Shield projection towers

⬇ Turbolaser tower batteries were the most elevated structures of the Death Star's city sprawls.

The long trenches that cut across the Death Star's surface at right angles contained service ports, docking bays and hangars, and also vents and ports for expelling built-up heat. Typical trenches stretched for many kilometers in a straight line, and some circumnavigated the entire sphere. The most prominent trench wrapped around the battle station's equator.

Major and minor trenches were used by pilots of shuttles and starfighters as directional markers. Because traveling via shuttle between distant zones on the Death Star was often more efficient than traveling via turbolifts, shuttle pilots also used the major trenches as flight paths.

While low-energy shield projectors covered the many access and disposal ports in the trenches, the main source of protection came from the XX-9 heavy turbolaser towers that were positioned along the top of the trenches as well as along the trench floors. The trenches' defensive systems were programmed to prevent the turbolaser batteries from accidentally blasting each other or damaging the station's hull and surface structures.

Major trenches divided numerous city sprawls, but

→ An aerial view of the latitudinal trench that traversed the Death Star's north pole.

↓ The battle station's latitudinal trench was wide enough to accommodate three single-pilot starfighters in attack formation.

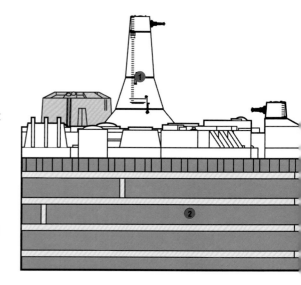

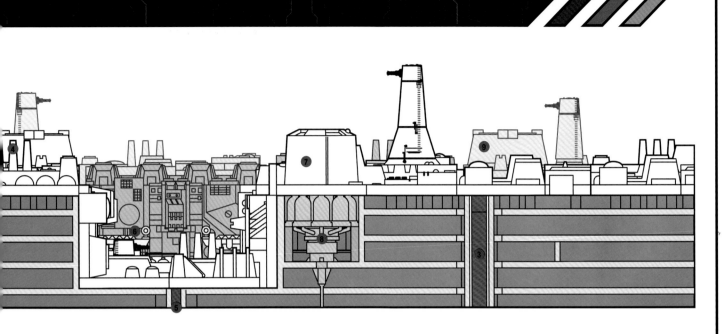

some minor trenches traversed sprawls. Maintenance crews used tractor beams to ensure that jettisoned trash would not fall back or drift into any trenches.

Although the Death Star's designers were aware of the fact that the trenches were accessible to enemy starfighters, they were confident that such an attack could be readily defeated by Imperial firepower, and would not cause significant damage.

1 **Turbolaser tower**
2 **Sub-surface levels**
3 **Turbolift shaft**
4 **Communications array**
5 **Thermal exhaust shaft**
6 **Ray shield projectors**
7 **Shield projection tower**
8 **Shield generator**

9 **Defense-field generator**
10 **Power distribution nodes**
11 **Service access port**
12 **Shuttle landing pad**
13 **Cosmic ray sink**
14 **Sensor suite field**
15 **Energy flush vent**
16 **Heat sink**

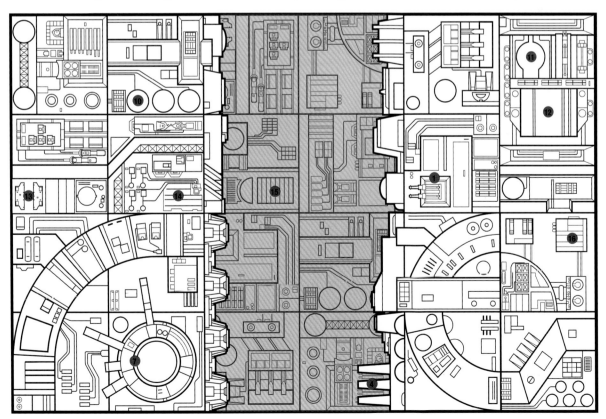

All of the operating forces stationed in North 7: A68 resided in a large general quarters building. Living quarters ranged from austere barracks for the crew to multi-room luxury apartments for the senior officers. Lower officers shared their quarters with as many as three other officers of the same rank, while higher officers received private quarters. The crew quarters bunked as many as 50 individuals per room, but combat pilots and highly-skilled technical crew members received better accommodations than the average service tech.

In addition to living quarters, the general quarters building had recreational areas, mess halls, and sport courts. Maintenance and management of general quarters fell to Battle Station Operations, but the building was divided into areas where army and navy operations had jurisdiction, and their own respective support personnel monitored the activities of the crew and officers.

The crew ate in a large, open room full of tables and benches. Meal trays were delivered by droids, and the fare was cultivated from the Death Star's food and water synthesization plants. The officer mess halls featured more secluded dining facilities, and the food came from the huge stores of refrigerated and dried goods imported by Imperial cargo ships.

→ Imperial officers were quartered close to their stormtrooper barracks in their sectors, allowing the officers to summon and mobilize the troops quickly.

→ Except for when they were asleep or assigned to individual sentry posts, stormtroopers were rarely alone in any area of the Death Star.

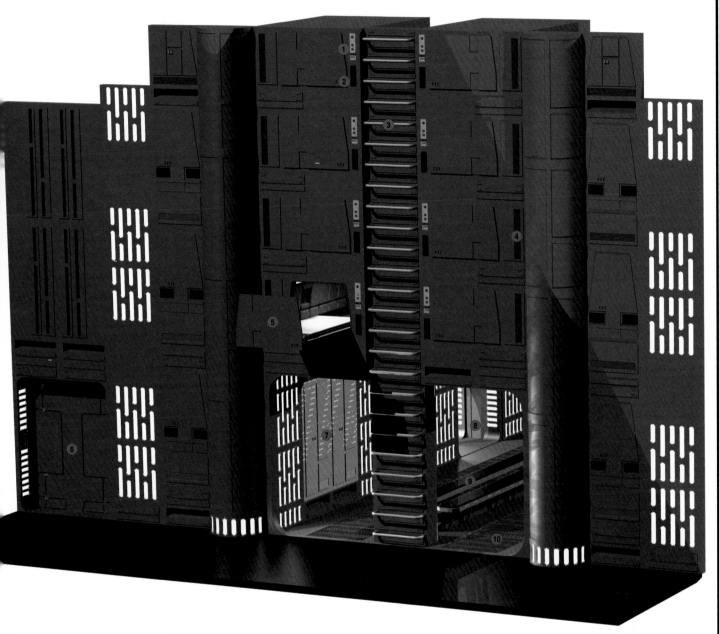

STORMTROOPER BARRACKS

Taking inspiration from barracks used by Republic Army clone troopers during the Clone Wars, the Death Star's designers created ladder-accessible enclosed chambers for stormtroopers. Each chamber held a single, extendible bunk, and was equipped with a viewscreen, comlink, controls for lighting and air conditioning, and built-in sensors that allowed stormtrooper squad leaders, droid medical teams, and Imperial Intelligence agents to monitor the stormtroopers. If Imperial Intelligence had reason to suspect a stormtrooper was a Rebel Alliance agent,

they were authorized to use remote controls to lock the stormtrooper within his chamber. Stormtroopers placed their armor and weapons in lockers before ascending to their respective bunks.

1. **Bunk control panel**
2. **Trooper ID plate**
3. **Bunk access ladder**
4. **Independent air handler**
5. **Open trooper bunk**
6. **Refresher**
7. **Gear lockers**
8. **To sonic showers**
9. **Benches**
10. **Ventilated flooring**

RECREATION FACILITIES

→ A Stormtrooper takes aim with a BlasTech SE-14r light repeating blaster.

The Death Star's recreation areas typically consisted of a main chamber filled with running tracks, weight-training machines, calisthenic and aerobic training space, martial-arts sparring areas, and other personal exercise stations. Side chambers featured lockers and sonic showers, holo obstacle and combat training simulation facilities, equipment and exercise droid storage, refreshment bars, multipurpose sport courts, puttie course, and recreation staff offices.

Every member of the Death Star's crew was encouraged to use the exercise equipment. To maintain their fighting skills and learn new techniques, all crew members were periodically assigned to the combat training and obstacle course facilities. Combat training included refresher courses in handling blasters, grenades, and heavy weapons, and lessons or assigned instructions in melee and biological weapons. The obstacle course's computer held programs that generated an endlessly expandable variety of holographic representations of terrain and situations, all engineered to test the crew's limits of ability and ingenuity.

↓ A selection of blasters issued aboard the Death Star and used regularly in combat training.

The recreation facilities' refreshment bars served healthy drinks that replenished vitamins and vital fluids lost after a strenuous workout or examination. The sport courts could be configured for playing various popular games, including wallball, kel tag, and repulsor puck.

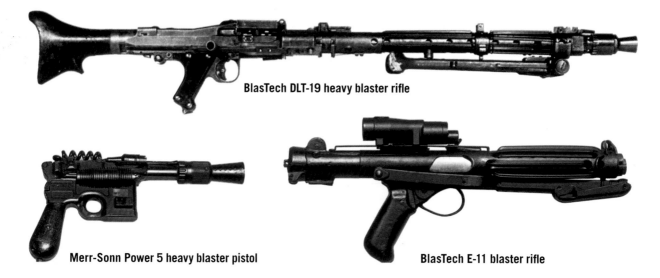

BlasTech DLT-19 heavy blaster rifle

Merr-Sonn Power 5 heavy blaster pistol

BlasTech E-11 blaster rifle

1. Lift to track
2. To refreshment bar
3. Sparring courts
4. Melee training lane
5. Benches
6. Exercise stations
7. To showers/lockers
8. Calisthenics area
9. Weight machines
10. Elevated track
11. Chief trainer's office
12. Refresher
13. Maintenance office
14. Holo obstacle &
     combat simulation
15. Multipurpose courts
16. Equipment room
17. Practice range
18. Range office
19. Turbolift cluster
20. Shaft

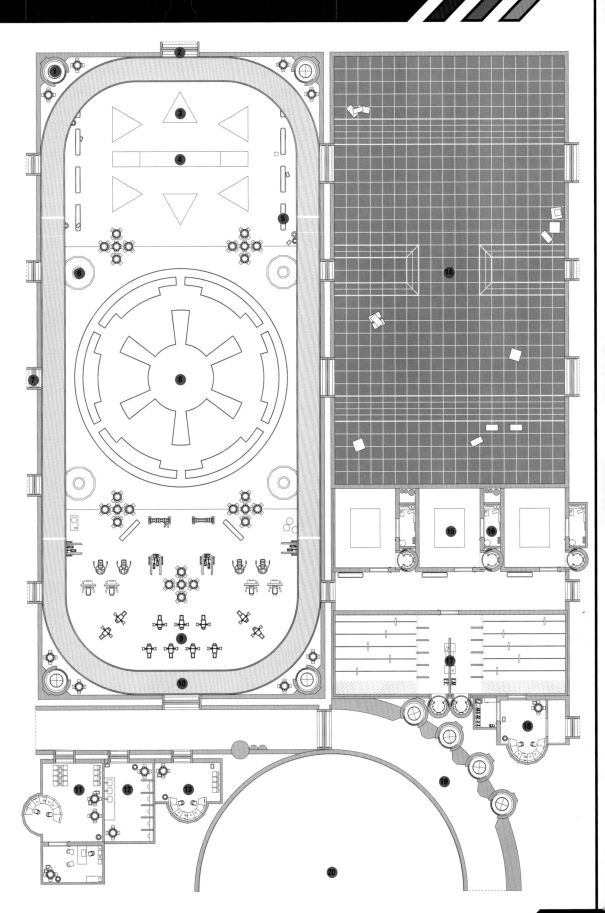

TURBOLIFTS

Turbolift conveyances utilize repulsorlift field generators—the most common form of technology in the galaxy—to transport passengers through architectural shafts or hollow tubes. By filling long stretches of crisscrossing cylindrical shafts with repulsor fields, Bevel Lemelisk's design team created an efficient travel system that connected all sectors of the battle station.

On any given level of the Death Star, turbolift conveyances were positioned every few hundred meters and typically in clusters to guarantee at least one turbolift car would always be waiting for Imperial personnel. Turbolift cars raced at incredible speeds, and could cover many kilometers per minute. Despite the speed and availability of the cars, it was often faster and more convenient to take a shuttle from one hangar bay to another that was close to the final destination, especially when traveling between different zones on the surface of the Death Star.

The turbolift cars were engineered to rotate, which was necessary because most of the battle station's inner gravity orientation transitions were accomplished by turbolifts. During transit, the car rotated to match the orientation of the destination deck, while compensators

→ A cross-sectional turbolift map illustrates the major routes within zones 3 and 9. Knowing that shuttles would be a more efficient mode of transport between widely separated sections of the Death Star, the designers incorporated lift tubes that led directly to shuttle systems.

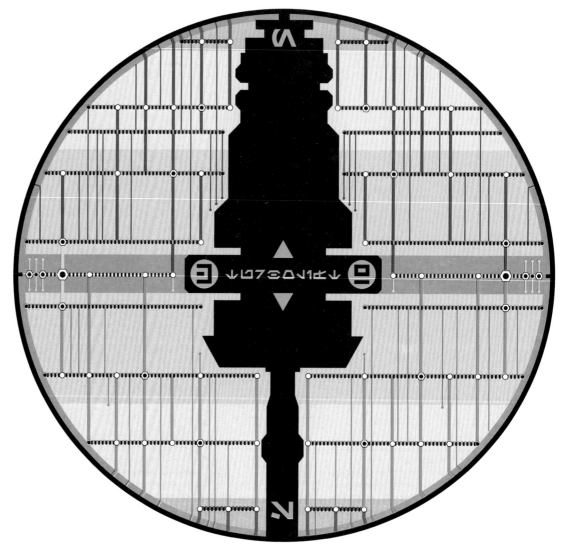

	LATERAL SHUTTLE SYSTEM		CONNECTION POINT TO CONCENTRIC SHUTTLE SYSTEM
	EQUATORIAL LIFTS		
	NORTHERN HEMISPHERE LIFTS		
	SOUTHERN HEMISPHERE LIFTS		CONNECTION POINT TO LATERAL SHUTTLE SYSTEM
	POLAR REGION LIFTS		

kept passengers comfortable and unaware of any change in gravity orientation.

Turbolift cars were activated by voice command, but access to certain areas of the Death Star required a rank cylinder key, as such areas were limited to specific crew designations and ranks. If a crewman requested a turbolift car to take him to an area that was closed to his classification, and he failed to provide a rank cylinder key, the turbolift's computer would prevent the car from moving. If the requested destination was an especially sensitive area, the computer would inform security of the crewman's possible intent to trespass.

1 **Upper repulsor**
2 **Orientation sensors**
3 **Power charge coils**
4 **Magnetic guide rails**
5 **Outer doors (open)**
6 **Artificial gravity plate**
7 **Repulsor lift**
8 **Emergency mag-brake**

↓ **Executive lift tubes were reserved for Darth Vader and high-ranking officers. Concealed scanners and security devices prevented unauthorized use.**

↘ **Rebel authorities have confirmed the stormtroopers in this image were actually Luke Skywalker and Han Solo, accompanied by their 'captive', Chewbacca.**

CORRIDORS

The Death Star's gray-and-black corridors appeared strictly utilitarian, but were actually part of the battle station's complex network of linked systems. Energy from the station's reactor was channeled through and around the corridors to provide power for lighting, ventilation, and air-conditioning, and was also utilized for the station's artificial gravity systems.

Gravity within the station was maintained by omni-directional gravity boosters built into decks, walls, and ceilings. Easily adjustable gravity boosters were designed to allow gravity orientation to be altered from sector to sector, or even corridor to corridor. While hangar bays imposed gravity perpendicular to the battle station's core, adjoining corridors shifted the gravity orientation toward the core. To prevent accidents, numerous warning signs were activated when the gravity orientation changed from one section to the next.

The corridors were designed not only for pedestrian access throughout the battle station but also for military drilling exercises. At any given time, patrols of stormtroopers could be found marching on various levels of every zone while security personnel used restricted corridors to test their weapons and scanners in mock hunts for rebel interlopers.

① **Luminous conduits**   ④ **Air vents**
② **Light diffuser**   ⑤ **Air return**
③ **Perforated front panel**   ⑥ **Power lines**

➜ Always on the lookout for saboteurs and rebel insurgents, Imperial stormtroopers were an intimidating presence as they marched through the Death Star's corridors.

BLAST DOORS

The Death Star was equipped with two types of doors: regular doors, which were generally found between rooms and corridors in general quarters areas, and blast doors, which separated corridors from command centers, docking bays, and adjoining corridors. Both types retracted into walls, ceilings, and floors. Blast doors utilized magnetic seals, making them virtually impossible to unlock without proper authorization codes, and were impervious to standard blaster fire.

The Death Star's security personnel issued rank cylinders to Imperial officers and crew members. Rank cylinders allowed users to access secured areas and doors, as well as to navigate and access information from the Imperial computer network. Stormtroopers used their comlinks to contact security officers when they required blast doors to be opened or closed at specific locations.

Blast doors that separated docking bays from corridors were well guarded, and could be opened and closed remotely by the docking-bay control room, and also by way of consoles on the walls beside the doors. The docking bay blast doors were reinforced to protect the rest the station from potentially dangerous cargoes.

← Wide blast doors retracted into doorways and separated corridors at practical and strategic intersections. To trap or eliminate trespassers, corridors could be rapidly sealed, locked, and depressurized.

← Recovered from a military communications complex on Galvoni III, recordings from a Death Star security camera yielded images of two interlopers making a narrow escape through a closing blast door.

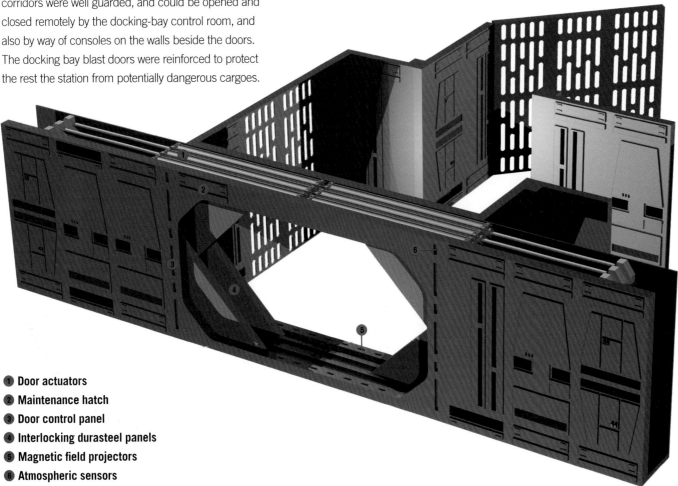

1 **Door actuators**
2 **Maintenance hatch**
3 **Door control panel**
4 **Interlocking durasteel panels**
5 **Magnetic field projectors**
6 **Atmospheric sensors**

Numerous areas throughout the Death Star consisted of vast air shafts. These shafts helped circulate air, pressurize the battle station's habitable sections, and also channeled heat that expended from generators located within the shafts. All shafts incorporated Imperial-designed superannuated System Four ventilation systems, and were built in compliance with Imperial standards.

Death Star personnel could traverse the air shafts via extendible bridges, which retracted into the shaft walls. Controls for the bridges were built into the frames of doorways for bridge-access areas. Although most bridges were wide enough to allow at least two personnel to walk abreast, few bridges had protective railings, as they were conceived specifically for use by Imperial stormtroopers and ambulatory service and maintenance droids, who by their respective training and programming did not experience vertigo. Imperial officers and other crew members typically avoided the bridges, and claimed the lift tubes were a much more efficient mode of transportation within the station.

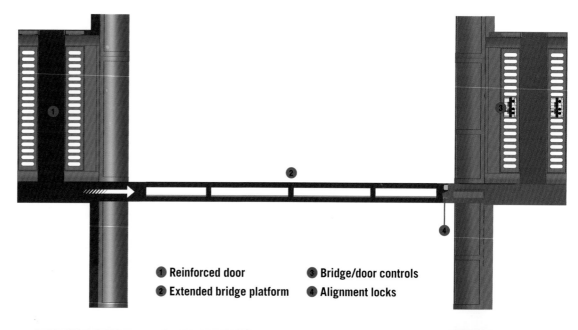

1 **Reinforced door**
2 **Extended bridge platform**
3 **Bridge/door controls**
4 **Alignment locks**

➜ Recovered from an Imperial communications complex on Galvoni III, this image shows Princess Leia Organa and Luke Skywalker on the edge of a retracted bridge in the Death Star's central core shaft.

↑ After a group of rebels infiltrated the Death Star's central core shaft, stormtroopers took advantage of upper-level hatches as strategic firing points.

↓ Kuat PJC 223 power generators were mounted to the walls of the Death Star's central core shaft. Imperial designers were only concerned by the functionality and structural integrity of the generators, and never imagined that the units' lower pipes might provide trespassers with an opportunity for escape.

1 Maintenance hatch
2 Controls to extend bridge
3 Reinforced door
4 Magnetic alignment pins
5 Non-slip plating
6 Edge safety sensors
7 Retracted bridge
8 Bridge alignment locks

SECURITY SECTOR

Recovered Imperial Datafile #003729.61v: Grand Moff Tarkin's introductory address to Death Star Security Officers

As you all have access to Imperial personnel records, I must assume that you are familiar with certain details of my own military career, that long before my appointment to this battle station, I was the Republic Outland Regions Security Force Commander. I mention this to assure you that I am more than well aware of your duties and responsibilities as members of the Death Star's security sector.

I have always maintained that the primary purpose of security is to maintain the peace. But as security officers, I expect you to not only honor the rules and regulations of the Imperial military establishment but also adhere to proper decorum at all times, especially when maintaining the security of high-ranking officers and visiting officials.

I must stress that the Death Star is not just a battle station, but a community comprised of hundreds of neighborhoods. The survival of the community depends upon its members getting along and working together smoothly.

Unfortunately, all communities suffer some level of tension and personal violence. Should any crewmember stray from their duties, or any officer abuse the power entrusted to him, I expect the surveillance branch to report such transgressions to the wardens immediately. Should an argument or discussion between crewmembers get, shall we say, out of hand, I fully expect the enforcement wardens to put down the disturbance and restore order.

← Darth Vader leads a contingent of Imperial officers through a security sector on the Death Star.

Charged with patrolling and guarding vital or off-limits areas aboard the Death Star, Imperial security officers—known throughout the Empire as wardens—also maintained the detention cell blocks, policed corridors, and protected visiting officials. Wardens were among the only Imperial officers on the battle station to carry personal weapons at all times. They were assigned to several different security divisions, including enforcement, protection, surveillance, and detention.

The surveillance division worked with enforcement and protection to create a complete umbrella of security aboard the battle station. Relying on a myriad of hidden cameras, sensors, mobile remotes and droids, surveillance stations remained on alert throughout all duty shifts.

The wardens themselves were under constant surveillance and observation, as each standard security sector was required to provide office space and reasonable assistance to the Imperial Security Bureau (ISB). The ISB served as a fact-finding and special-assignments division of the Imperial bureaucracy, and was represented by agents who specialized in surveillance, investigations, internal affairs, interrogation, re-education, and enforcement. Because the ISB's policing and surveillance techniques were even more harsh than typical Imperial security standards, and because they were known to place undercover agents among military and technical-support personnel, security forces throughout the Empire maintained a tense relationship with the ISB.

Each security sector maintained its own armory store. Amories contained a wealth of weapons, ammunition, and protective gear. Blaster pistols and rifles, grenades, mounted laser cannons, melee weapons, and body armor were typically stored behind locked blast doors. Turbolifts delivered security personnel to larger armories that were connected to nearby hangar bays, and which held the Army's land combat vehicles, including AT-AT walkers and repulsortanks.

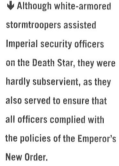

↓ Although white-armored stormtroopers assisted Imperial security officers on the Death Star, they were hardly subservient, as they also served to ensure that all officers complied with the policies of the Emperor's New Order.

Imperial scanning crews used portable equipment that included an Idellian Arrays ILF-4500-2 life-form scanner. More sophisticated than the Death Star's military-grade long-range sensors, the ILF-4500-2 can more readily detect concealed life forms.

→ The floor plan of Security Sector N7: A68-1 was typical of similar facilities on the Death Star.

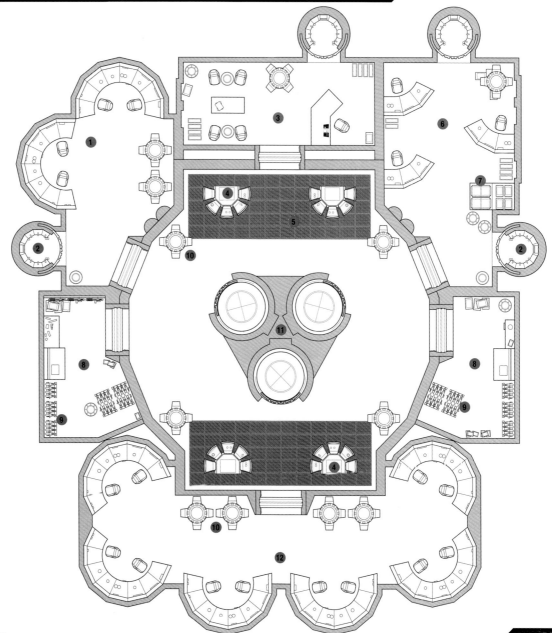

1. **Watch stations**
2. **Circuitry bay**
3. **Imperial Security Bureau office**
4. **Guard posts**
5. **Grated flooring**
6. **Security office**
7. **Equipment rack**
8. **Armory**
9. **Blaster rifle racks**
10. **Power units**
11. **Turbolift cluster**
12. **Surveillance stations**

DETENTION BLOCK AA-23

Detention was the branch of security that maintained the Death Star's detention blocks which held individuals who had been charged for infractions. Typical 'guests' in the detention block cells included political prisoners, criminals, saboteurs, and Imperial personnel who disobeyed orders.

Detention blocks were located away from the main command and personnel areas in the Death Star, and were accessible by turbolifts. Like most chambers in the battle station, the walls were dark gray metal, but the floors were grilled and illuminated by red lights. Detention wardens and guards were stationed in the block's control room, and were trained to handle prisoners and maintain their cells. Cells had magnetic-locked doors and extremely utilitarian interiors, consisting of little more than bare-metal walls and a built-in metal bench.

The guard stations in the control room held monitors linked to wall and ceiling-mounted holocam units, which kept a constant watch over everyone and every movement in the block's workstations. The security cameras were in turn linked to wall-mounted BlasTech Class VI automated laser projectors, and fed targeting data to the laser's combat computer. Beyond the control room, a flight of steps ascended to the cell bay, a long corridor lined with cell doors.

The grilled floors were engineered so that the entire cell bay, including the cells themselves, could be sluiced out automatically, removing all traces of blood and other unpleasant by-products of torture and terror. Grills were also located along the side of the corridor to allow the waste to exit.

1 **Multi-dimensional cameras**　**4** **Audio sensor**
2 **Thermographic sensor**　**5** **Lens plate**
3 **Status indicator lights**　**6** **Mounting plate**

⬇ Imperial records confirmed the identity of Lieutenant Shann Childsen (foreground), who was in charge of the Imperial wardens in the control room of Detention Block AA-23. Armed with blaster pistols, wardens monitored prisoners, maintained authority, and prevented escapes.

→ Ceiling-mounted automated holocam units recorded all proceedings within the battle station's detention block and transmitted visual and audio data to each zone's command sector authority.

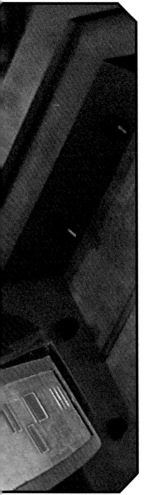

← This image of rebel infiltrators attacking a Death Star detention block was recovered from a transmission to the Imperial communications complex on Galvoni III.

← The Death Star's detention block walls were lined with embedded BlasTech Class VI automated laser projectors. Nicknamed laser traps, these automated blasters were typically found in Imperial prisons and labor camps, where they were used to suppress inmate uprisings.

The most common droid aboard the Death Star was the MSE-6 general-purpose droid. Each MSE-6 is a Class-3 droid equipped with a single modular circuit matrix that can hold only one skill at a time, but the matrices are inexpensive and so easy to install that one MSE-6 can reprogram another without difficulty. Standard MSE-6 skill matrices include elementary repair, security checks, message delivery, janitorial cleanup, and basic computer programming.

The MSE-6 was introduced years ago by the now-defunct Chadra-Fan company Rebaxan Columni. Chadra-Fan engineers patterned the MSE-6 after the pleeky, a diminutive pet animal from their homeworld, Chad III, and were so confident that the droid would appeal to countless consumers that they manufactured hundreds of billions of units. Unfortunately, consumers from dozens of worlds quickly realized that the small, scurrying droids and their audiocast patterns resembled various species of disease-carrying vermin, and Rebaxan Columni was inundated with billions of returns and requests for refunds. The company managed to stave off bankruptcy by offering a cut-rate deal on the entire production run to the Republic Army and Navy, who needed the droids for their warships. Subsequently, MSE-6s were adopted by the Imperial Army and Navy, and can be found on nearly every Imperial vessel and station.

The MSE-6's outer casing can conceal two retractable manipulator arms, one for heavy-duty work and the other for delicate operations. A sensitive auditory sensor is located on either side of the casing, and an electro-photoreceptor and miniature holocam are located on the front. When the MSE-6 is used a courier, it utilizes a small compartment to hold sealed orders and classified documents. Once locked, the compartment cannot be opened without an authorized voice-code.

The MSE-6 travels on a maneuverable set of treaded wheels and can move forward and backward quite rapidly. Despite their inflexible programming and propensity to flee from almost any unfamiliar noise, the Empire relied upon the droids to guide troops through the Death Star's labyrinthine corridors. These droids were also routinely sent into the battle station's ventilation ducts to inspect damage from mynock infestations and to drive off the energy-eating creatures.

➜ Staying close to walls in Death Star corridors, MSE droids formed trains to conserve energy, maintain orderly lines of travel, and avoid collisions with other droids and Imperial personnel.

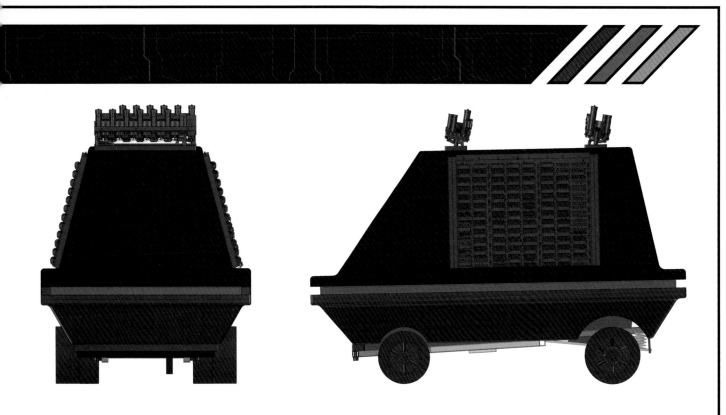

1. Encoded order/command cylinders
2. Mission sub-processor module
3. Logic processor module
4. Command processor module
5. Acoustic navigation sensors
6. Electrophoto sensor band
7. General diagnostic port
8. Holo-encoder cartridge
9. Protective casing
10. Environmental imager

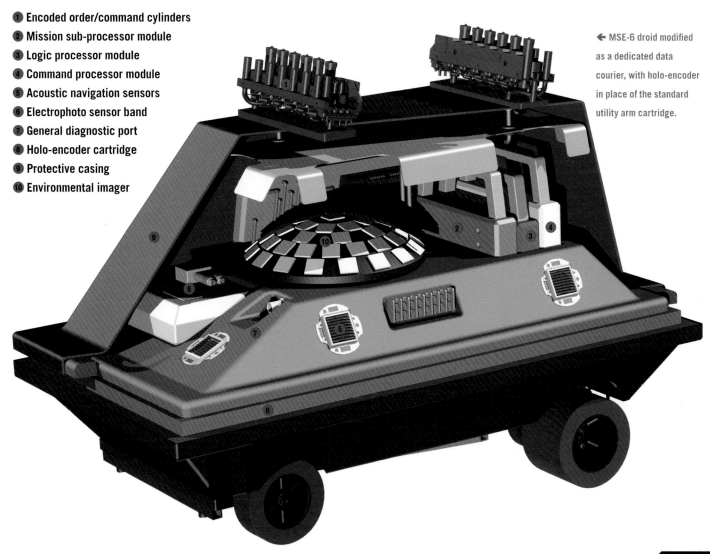

← MSE-6 droid modified as a dedicated data courier, with holo-encoder in place of the standard utility arm cartridge.

IT-O INTERROGATOR DROID

Developed by the Imperial Security Bureau, the IT-O interrogator droid uses numerous tools of torture to obtain information from enemies of the Empire.

The spherical droid, less than a meter in diameter, is encased in a glossy black shell, and hovers above the ground on low-power repulsors. Its surface is studded with an array of needles, probes, optic sensors, and audio receptors. Although the droid is equipped with a vocabulator capable of producing speech, the droid typically serves as a silent partner to an Imperial Security Bureau agent or other personnel authorized to question prisoners.

In designing the IT-O, Imperial engineers incorporated technology from top-of-the-line medical droids as well as ultra-secret assassin droids. Like medical droids, the IT-O has sophisticated medical diagnostic matrices and expert programming in medicine, psychology, surgery, and humanoid biology. However, instead of analyzing what is wrong with a body system, the IT-O attempts to discover how to make a healthy system go wrong. Its vital-sign monitors make it capable of predicting and preventing the onset of catalepsy or unconsciousness, enabling the droid to bring prisoners back from the brink of death so they can endure further questioning.

A hypodermic injector syringe, deliberately oversized to inspire anxiety and fear, is one of the droid's most prominent devices. The needle dispenses a variety of liquid chemicals that are stored in internal reservoirs. These drugs can lower pain thresholds, stimulate cooperation, and trigger hallucinations. The most frequently used drug is the remarkably effective truth serum Bavo Six.

The IT-O also features a laser scalpel, a grasping claw, and power shears. Not surprisingly, the very sight of an IT-O is sufficient to frighten most prisoners into divulging secrets and submitting admissions of guilt. The droid's sensors can easily analyze a prisoner's heart rate, muscle tension, and voice patterns to evaluate whether the prisoner has told the truth. Despite the Imperial Security Bureau's boasts about the effectiveness of their interrogation droids, it is possible for strong-willed subjects to withstand the torments of an IT-O.

⬇ Darth Vader used an IT-O droid to interrogate Princess Leia Organa on the Death Star. Image obtained from the Imperial communications complex on Galvoni III.

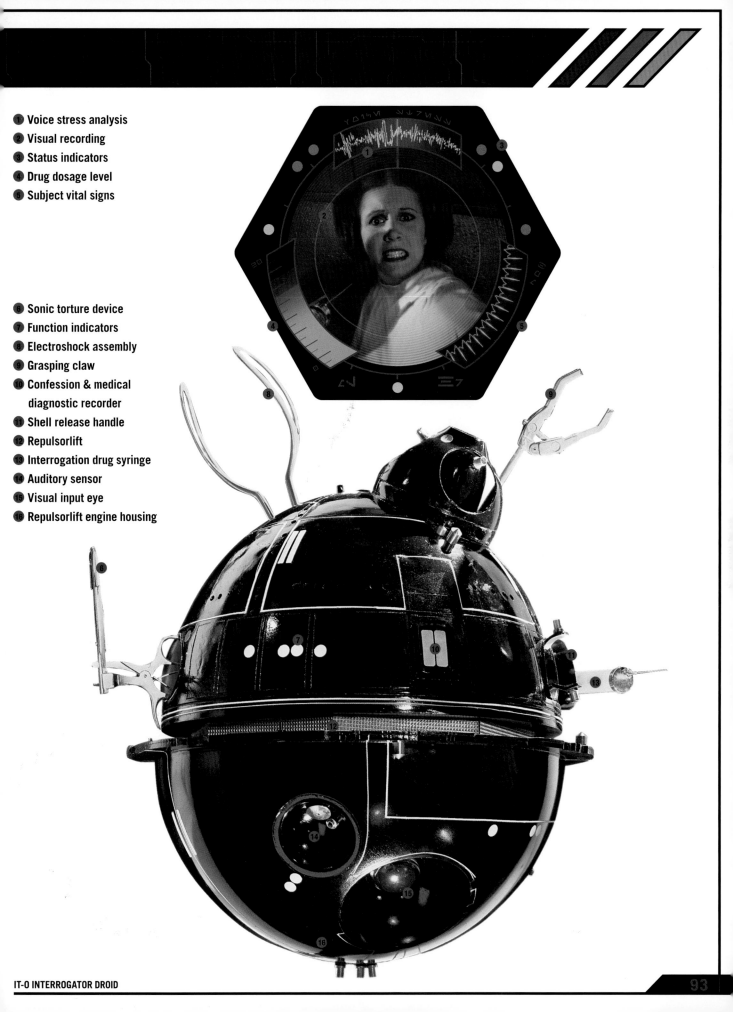

1. Voice stress analysis
2. Visual recording
3. Status indicators
4. Drug dosage level
5. Subject vital signs

6. Sonic torture device
7. Function indicators
8. Electroshock assembly
9. Grasping claw
10. Confession & medical diagnostic recorder
11. Shell release handle
12. Repulsorlift
13. Interrogation drug syringe
14. Auditory sensor
15. Visual input eye
16. Repulsorlift engine housing

SERVICE & TECHNICAL SECTORS

Personal Data Journal Entry #478,
Grand Moff Tarkin recording

Recent exchanges with **Chief Lemelisk** have made it abundantly clear to me that the Death Star's ongoing service and technical requirements will require even more personnel than originally projected. Constructing a superweapon for the Empire may be our primary goal, but of tantamount importance is the need to maintain the battle station's thousands of kilometers of maintenance tunnels, accessways, trash compactors, and ventilation ducts. These areas will be the domain of the service sector, and the more I think of it, the more convinced I am that service shall be the true backbone of the station's operation.

Service technicians will spend the bulk of their duty time inspecting, maintaining, repairing, and replacing machinery. From highly-skilled technicians trained to build components from scratch, to almost-mindless droids programmed to clean corridors, service will likely be taken for granted by other sectors. Though it seems unlikely that any number of rebel attacks could ever cause a significant hull breach, the service sector's most important duty may be the upkeep of the station's protective and emergency gear.

As for the technicians who won't be part of the service sector, they shall be assigned to the technical sector, and work in the science stations, medical bays, research laboratories, programming facilities, and engineering sections. While it's hard to imagine a weapon more destructive than the superlaser, I imagine the technical sector may eventually be tasked with developing an even more powerful weapon.

However, the service and technical sector must never be allowed to become deluded into thinking they are somehow *more* important than the military sector. Their strength is not in their numbers or capabilities, but in their service to the Empire. And more specifically, in their services to the Death Star.

← Imperial astromech droids were stationed in
all hangars and docking bays on the Death Star.

Every general sector on the Death Star had at least several maintenance areas. A typical maintenance section within a sprawl featured a series of connected repair stations, a storage warehouse full of spare parts, monitoring stations which received continual diagnostic reports and could hook into a droid's visual sensors, and machinery for repairing worn components or even constructing new components from raw materials.

All corridors and duty stations contained concealed but easily accessible emergency equipment that had to be charged with power or replaced on a regular basis. A standard emergency gear locker contained breath masks, environmental suits, food, water rations, glow rods, location beacons, laser cutters, and comlinks. Anticipating the possibility that a hull rupture could leave some personnel unable to reach escape pods, the Death Star's service sector made sure each emergency gear locker also contained temporary environment pouches. Using these pouches personnel would be able to survive the breach of space for up to 12 hours.

When service techs were not busy performing repairs or routine maintenance on the Death Star's machinery, they were stationed at monitoring posts, where they checked temperature and performance readings or waited for system-failure alarms to sound. All machinery was installed with built-in diagnostic systems that fed performance information to the monitors in maintenance. These readings measured coolant levels, air quality, noise output, heat generations, and a score of other indications that were constantly compared to factory norms and Imperial standards. Any significant dips or rises in the data resulted in warning sensors alerting on-duty techs to make more detailed investigations.

⬇ An image obtained from an Imperial communications complex revealed Imperial MSE droids with a motley assortment of droids in Maintenance Section 19-52. Rebel allies identified the non-Imperial droids as property stolen from Jawas on Tatooine.

Vehicle maintenance shops were located on the decks below and around the latitude hangar bays. Every bay had a lift that lowered spacecraft either directly into a waiting shop or to a repulsor shaft that connected to a shop. Maintenance crews and droids cleaned carbon buildup, changed components, and overhauled engines. The shops provided routine tune-ups and overhauls for Imperial starfighters, strike cruisers, and shuttles, and were equipped with parts and materials to repair damaged spacecraft.

DEATH STAR DROIDS

Manufactured by Arakyd Industries, the RA-7 protocol droid was conceived to serve Imperial officers. The Imperial Security Bureau ordered thousands of RA-7s, and installed sophisticated programming to enable the droids to be used as spies. Although RA-7s were outnumbered by MSE droids on the Death Star, they became known as Death Star Droids because of their ubiquitous presence in all areas of the battle station, including maintenance sections.

⬇ Death Star service technicians were expected to maintain everything from Imperial probe droids to TIE fighter pilot gear.

1. **Magnetic sensor**
2. **Broadband photoreceptors**
3. **Resonating vocabulator**
4. **Interface connection port**
5. **Advanced auditory sensors**
6. **Magnetic-grip foot plates**

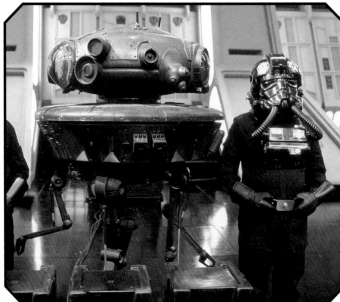

The Death Star was in every way a warship, but the designers did not overlook the need for medical facilities to ensure the Imperial crew and soldiers remained healthy and fit for duty, and also to administer treatment to those who were injured during their service. A typical facility was Medical Station 381-N3, which was staffed by medical technicians of varying rank and ability, and by droids that specialized in medical techniques, including surgery, anesthesia, and prosthetics.

Arranged around a convenient turbolift cluster, Medical Station 381-N3 featured large open chambers that served as either examination rooms or operating theaters. The chambers contained diagnostic examination platforms and operating tables, and each could be partitioned to form three separate rooms.

The Death Star reportedly carried large supplies of bacta, an exotic chemical compound that can heal almost any wound. While minor wounds could be treated with disposable patches coated with bacta gel, patients with more serious injuries were completely submersed in cylindrical bacta tanks. Medical Station 381-N3 had two bacta tank wards with a total of 16 bacta tanks, which were manufactured by Zaltin Baca Corporation.

Although the restorative properties of bacta remains the fastest and most effective method for healing, bacta baths were reserved for only the most seriously injured patients. Life-threatening injuries were handled by a special intensive care ward that combined bacta-tank treatments with life-support machinery. Non-life-threatening injuries were treated and the patients were sent to recuperation wards.

1. **Dividable exam room**
2. **To recuperation wards**
3. **Medical Officer station**
4. **Medical lab**
5. **Bacta tank wards**
6. **To command offices**
7. **Turbolift cluster**
8. **To intensive care ward**
9. **Medical duty station**
10. **Secure medical storage**
11. **Sterilization field**
12. **Dividable operating room**
13. **To general sector**

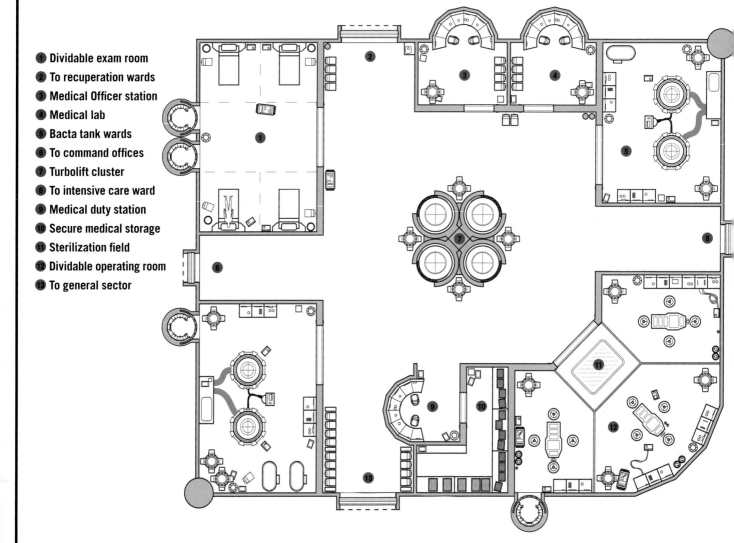

↑ During the Galactic Civil War, the Emperor forged alliances with two bacta corporations, Zaltin and Xucphra, making it nearly impossible for all but Imperial forces to acquire bacta.

↓ Manufactured by Medtech Industries, multi-armed FX-10 medical assistant droids were stationed in all Death Star medical stations.

← Medical droids on the Death Star included the Emdee series of diagnostic, laboratory technician, and microsurgery mechanicals.

① Multiwave visual sensors
② Hydraulic lines
③ Medical diagnostic computer
④ Computer interface socket
⑤ Servogrip pincers
⑥ Torso sheath
⑦ Hypodermic injector

WASTE REMOVAL

The Death Star's service sector was responsible for trash removal and processing. All personal quarters had their own refuse disposal points that fed into the larger chutes like tributaries into a river. Every corridor and room on the battle station had a trash disposal chute that led to a large waste-collection bin. Each city sprawl shared a single bin.

The entire process of waste management and disposal was controlled by central computer. Droids broke trash down, separating recyclable materials such as plastics, metal, food, and water from unrecyclable waste. Recyclable materials were sent for processing to the manufacturing centers within the zone or to the bulk storage and replication sections in the Death Star's deeper levels. Waste was directed through an elaborate system of garbage chutes and distributed into each zone's numerous trash compactors.

To maximize the amount of refuse that could be stored inside the compactors, the compactors' metal walls were designed to close together and crush trash into the smallest possible size. The compactors' maintenance hatches were magnetically sealed to prevent possibly toxic and combustible combinations of refuse from causing damage, and to prevent waste materials from leaking into outer chambers and nearby compartments. Despite the efforts at recycling, Imperials gave little thought to disposing of large, damaged girders and other construction materials, and tended to use the compactors like common dumpsters.

After being compacted, the trash would be moved to a jettison compartment along one of the trenches. As with other Imperial Navy vessels, the Death Star jettisoned unrecyclable trash immediately prior to hyperspace jumps.

⬇ Images obtained from an Imperial communications complex revealed Princess Leia Organa, Chewbacca the Wookiee, Han Solo, and Luke Skywalker landed within the confines of Death Star trash compactor 3263827 after their escape from Detention Block AA-23.

DIANOGA

Sometimes called 'garbage squid', dianoga evolved as marine scavengers on the swamp world Vordan. Ages ago, dianoga slithered into the hold of a space freighter, and the creatures quickly spread their populations to many planets. Thriving in sewers and river canals of large urban areas throughout the galaxy, dianoga feed on all types of refuse, and can consume almost anything except pure metals. A dianoga possesses seven tentacles used for locomotion and to catch food, and has a single, flexible eyestalk, which can extend around corners, or up like a periscope from underwater. Because dianogas can consume vast quantities of garbage, the Death Star's service sector not only tolerates their presence, but actually breeds them for use in the trash compactors.

↖ After a dianoga snared Luke Skywalker, Han Solo attempted to tug him free. The tentacled creature did not release Luke until the compactor walls began to move.

↑ In a desperate effort to stop the compactor's walls from converging, Princess Leia and her allies attempted to shift large pieces of scrap metal to jam the walls.

↓ Imperial technicians ignored scans of dianoga in the Death Star trash compactors because the creatures helped break down garbage and posed no threat.

COMMAND SECTOR

Excerpt from Personal Data Journal Entry #49, General Tagge of the Imperial Army recording

The Imperial command structure aboard the Death Star will be as strict as any organization found in the Empire. Command sectors will be found throughout the battle station, and will include many controls rooms. Imperial officers of no less than lieutenant rank shall supervise the command sectors.

The battle station will be under the command of a triumvirate headed by Grand Moff Tarkin, myself, and Admiral Motti of the Imperial Navy. The Chiefs of Navy, Army, and Battle Station Operations will be held by officers with the rank of colonel. Below each Operations Chief, eight majors will serve as chiefs of specific departments under heir branch of operations. In addition, four majors will be responsible for the general, service, technical, security, and military sectors. The military sectors will include Army troopers, the Navy's Death Star troopers, gunners, and pilots.

Two significant portions of the Death Star complement will not fall under the normal command structure, but are worth noting. The first is the Emperor's emissary, Lord Darth Vader, who will answer to Grand Moff Tarkin, and will not be subject to any other authority aboard the Death Star. Second, the Imperial stormtroopers. Both the Army and Navy may call upon the services of the stormtroopers, but with the firm understanding that these soldiers fall under the jurisdiction of neither, and that their primary loyalty is to the Emperor alone.

Although the Emperor rarely ventures from Coruscant, it is his decree that the Death Star must include a throne room. We must prepare this chamber with the full expectation that the Emperor will visit the battle station. The maintenance and management of the throne room shall also fall to the command sector.

⬅ When Emperor Palpatine was aboard the Death Star, his throne room was in every way the pinnacle of the command sector.

A vast command center that monitored all workstations and datafiles on the Death Star, the overbridge was the primary headquarters for the battle station's command triumvirate: Grand Moff Tarkin, General Tagge, and Admiral Motti. All information collected by the Death Star's bridges, sensor arrays, communication centers, and space traffic control was routed through the station's central computers and displayed on banks of monitors and holoprojectors situated throughout the overbridge. A secure holo communications booth allowed for private transmissions between the Grand Moff or Darth Vader and the Emperor.

Each member of the triumvirate had his own command station, and also stations for the operation chiefs at their respective services. They were assisted by lesser officers, droids, and enlisted crew who worked throughout each duty shift. In emergencies,

the overbridge could cut off all lesser command centers and control the entire Death Star.

Although the overbridge was quite capable of controlling the battle station during non-emergency situations as well, the triumvirate acknowledged it was more efficient to assign each zone's active bridge to be responsible for their own operations. Although the Death Star's designers believed it was highly unlikely that the overbridge could ever be damaged beyond repair, Emperor Palpatine insisted on a contingency plan for one of the

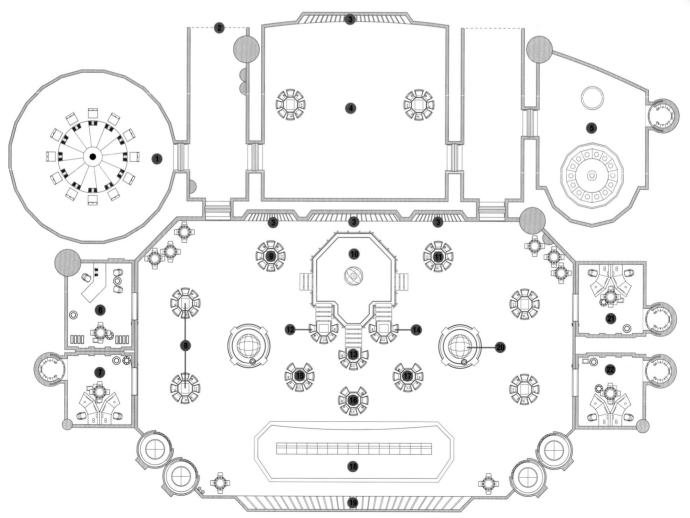

1. Conference room
2. To command staff offices
3. Viewscreens
4. Command sanctum
5. Secure holo booth
6. Grand Moff's office
7. Battle station operation's office
8. Duty posts
9. Security post
10. Command platform
11. Stormtrooper officer post
12. General's command station
13. Grand Moff's command station
14. Admiral's command station
15. Army operations chief
16. Battle station operations chief
17. Navy operations chief
18. Duty crew pit
19. Main viewscreen
20. Strategic holo display
21. Navy operation's office
22. Army operation's office

zone bridges or the throne room to assume control of the station. Only the Emperor's throne room could supersede the overbridge.

In addition to the operating officers and crew, 12 security officers and guards maintained posts on the overbridge to monitor the safety of the triumvirate. Sixteen stormtroopers were permanently assigned to the overbridge to maintain order and remind officers as well as crew that they all served the Emperor's will.

↑ The fortified command sanctum could be accessed only by the highest ranking officers during major station operations.

↓ Grand Moff Tarkin, Admiral Motti, Darth Vader, and General Tagge conferred on the Death Star's overbridge.

Adjacent to the Death Star's overbridge was a conference room with nearby offices for the command triumvirate and their aides. The conference room was used by the commanders to discuss daily operations as well as classified information. To ensure privacy, the rooms and offices were riddled with concealed sensors, sound dampeners, and frequency jammers that allowed conversation but effectively crippled any unauthorized transmissions or recordings.

To reach the conference room, one had to pass through four security points, each one requiring an increasing level of security clearance. Two guards remained in the room throughout meetings, quietly serving to remind delegates of the Imperial authority in charge.

Twelve seats ringed the room's large, circular table, which held embedded computer terminals and data displays. The terminals were used to brief commanders on battle tactics, and were linked to the Death Star's central command computers. A spherical holoprojector was located at the center of the table, and was used to display three-dimensional models of targets, planets, and enemy fleet formations.

Although a circular table in a conference room generally implies a degree of democracy, the Death Star's conference table had a strict seating hierarchy. The senior Imperial official, Grand Moff Tarkin, occupied a seat with an extended back. Those next in the chain of command would sit on either side of Tarkin, with the most junior officer seated opposite Tarkin at the bottom of the table. When Darth Vader attended such meetings, he rarely took a seat, and apparently preferred to remain standing.

A team of senior staff officers served as conference-room attendants. Responsible for preparing the room for meetings and keeping it spotless, they primed the terminals with necessary briefing notes, checked programming of holomodels, and executed thorough security sweeps prior to each meeting. During meetings, the attendants were stationed in a nearby room, ready to respond if summoned.

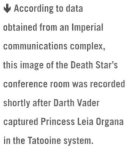

↓ According to data obtained from an Imperial communications complex, this image of the Death Star's conference room was recorded shortly after Darth Vader captured Princess Leia Organa in the Tatooine system.

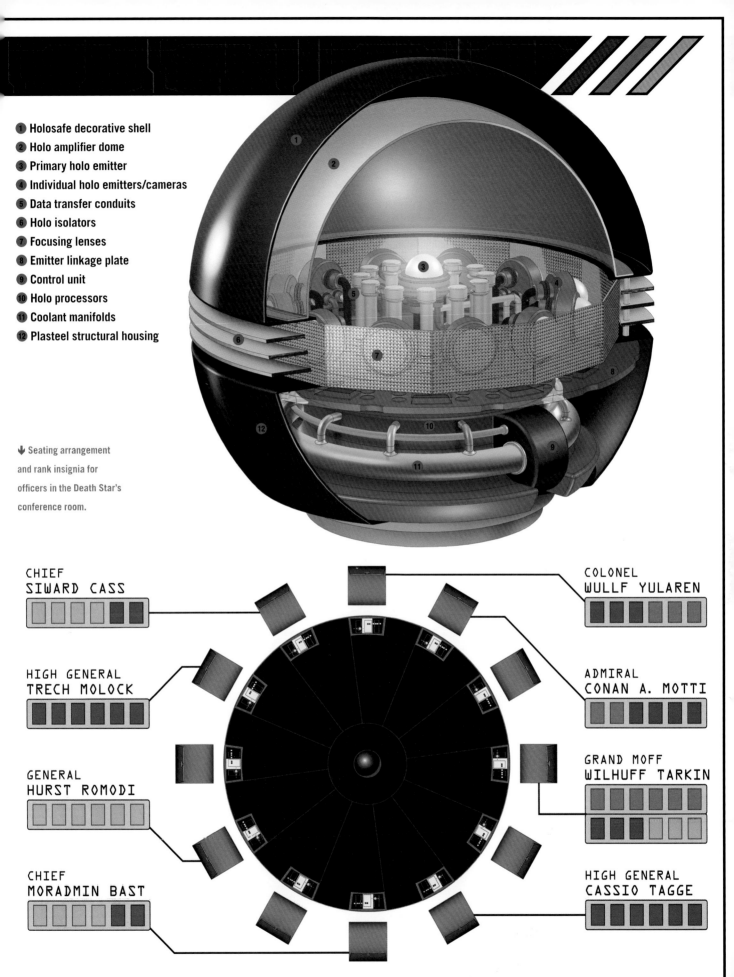

1. Holosafe decorative shell
2. Holo amplifier dome
3. Primary holo emitter
4. Individual holo emitters/cameras
5. Data transfer conduits
6. Holo isolators
7. Focusing lenses
8. Emitter linkage plate
9. Control unit
10. Holo processors
11. Coolant manifolds
12. Plasteel structural housing

↓ Seating arrangement
and rank insignia for
officers in the Death Star's
conference room.

CHIEF
SIWARD CASS

HIGH GENERAL
TRECH MOLOCK

GENERAL
HURST ROMODI

CHIEF
MORADMIN BAST

COLONEL
WULLF YULAREN

ADMIRAL
CONAN A. MOTTI

GRAND MOFF
WILHUFF TARKIN

HIGH GENERAL
CASSIO TAGGE

COMMAND SECTOR DUTY POSTS

➜ Imperial records confirmed the identity of Sergeant Jad Bean at a duty post in the Death Star's command center.

On the Death Star, any supervision station operated by an Imperial lieutenant or higher-ranking officer was designated a command sector duty post. A single duty post served as a "mini-bridge" for the commanding officer, the primary place from which he supervised his command and issued orders to his crew.

Each duty post console contained up to eight control boards, with four boards dedicated to the particular tasks assigned to the post. The remaining boards handled communications, damage and diagnostics, computer access, and a direct feed to the post's controlling bridge. Duty posts with eight control boards were designed with partially extendible frames that slid selected console modules aside to create a gap between modules, which enabled commanding officers to step in and out of their posts with ease.

Two to four security guards were stationed at typical command sector duty posts. Using the post's communications console, the commanding officer could summon additional guards, stormtroopers, and even Death Star troopers if the need arose.

➜ Sergeant Derek Torent, the senior watch trooper at the Death Star's command center, monitored external sensor data and scanned for Rebel Alliance activity.

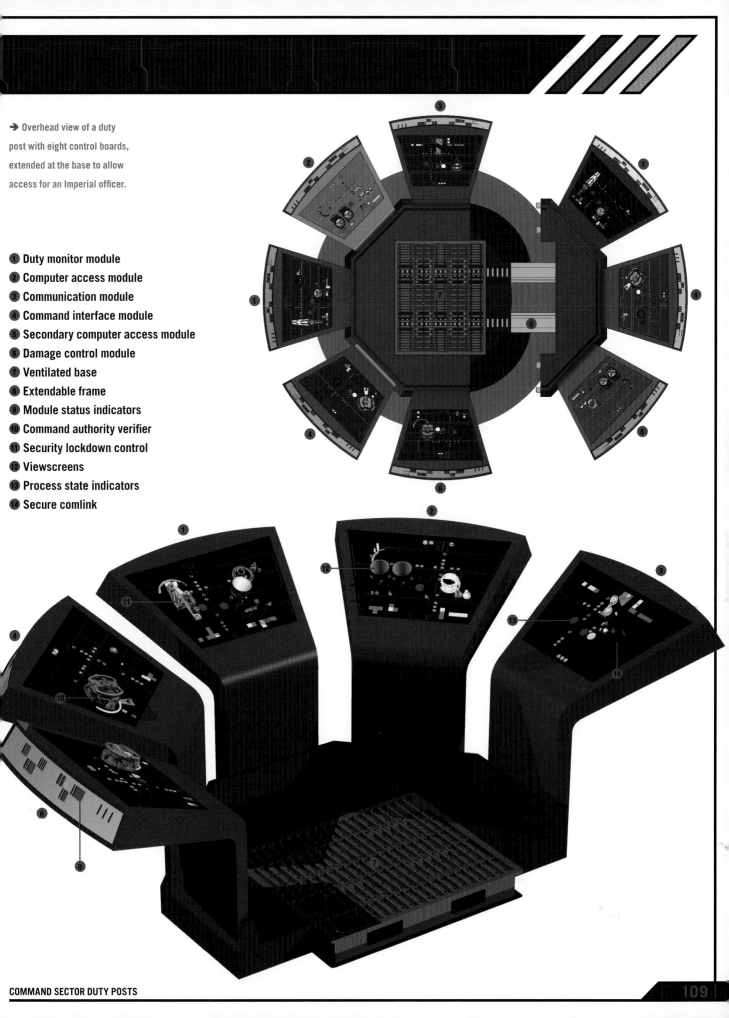

→ Overhead view of a duty post with eight control boards, extended at the base to allow access for an Imperial officer.

1. Duty monitor module
2. Computer access module
3. Communication module
4. Command interface module
5. Secondary computer access module
6. Damage control module
7. Ventilated base
8. Extendable frame
9. Module status indicators
10. Command authority verifier
11. Security lockdown control
12. Viewscreens
13. Process state indicators
14. Secure comlink

DEATH STAR II

Declassified message to Rebel Alliance leader
Princess Leia Organa, delivered via messenger
droid from Koth Melan, Assistant Consul
General for the Bothan Trade Mission:

"Greetings, Princess Leia. Koth Melan here, speaking to you from my homeworld of Bothawui. Our spy network has uncovered information vital to the Alliance, and the nature of these data are of such significance as to justify sending this messenger droid. You must come to Bothawui immediately. I cannot overemphasize the importance of this information, or the urgency. Time is of the essence. I will be at the Intergalactic Trade Mission for five days. The Alliance must act in that time or the information may be lost."

Excerpt from Princess Leia Organa's address
to fellow leaders of the Rebel Alliance:

"Koth Melan's Bothan agents discovered that the Empire has begun work on a new military project. The exact details are unknown, but according to Melan, the Emperor is diverting huge amounts of money, material, and men for this project. Unfortunately, the Bothans have been unable to pierce the cloud of secrecy that surrounds this matter.

"However, the agents have ascertained that the plans for this project are kept in the Emperor's computer vault on Coruscant, and that these plans will be copied onto another computer and transferred to Bothawui for dissemination to key personnel within the Imperial Intelligence community stationed there. If the Bothans can obtain this computer and crack its security codes, the Imperial secret will be laid bare.

"In case you're wondering, Koth Melan has not requested a fee for this information. Evidently, the Bothans are on our side."

← In its unfinished state in the remote Endor system, the
second Death Star did not appear to be an immediate threat
to the Rebel Alliance. However, both the construction status
and location of the Death Star were part of an elaborate trap
conceived by the Emperor himself.

After the destruction of the Death Star at Yavin, Emperor Palpatine ordered designer Bevel Lemelisk to produce an even more advanced battle station, with a hypermatter reactor able to generate power equivalent to hundreds of super-giant stars. The Emperor also demanded a faster hyperdrive for the new station.

Lemelisk immediately corrected the egregious flaws in the original design to leave no weak spots in the station's armor. Instead of relying on thermal exhaust ports to vent the reactor's incredible excess heat, the new station would instead funnel the waste energy through a series of millions of millimeter-wide heat dispersion ducts, which carried excess heat from the reactor core to the station's surface. If the ducts were hit during an attack, they were equipped with emergency baffles that were designed to muffle any high pulse of energy before it reached the core.

Lemelisk was also tasked with redesigning the station so its superlaser would deliver a more devastating blast, and have an increased rate of fire and greater accuracy.

While the first Death Star's superlaser required a recharge period of twenty-four hours, the second Death Star featured a superlaser that could be recharged in a matter of minutes. The superlaser's targeting and power-control systems were also refined so the weapon could be directed at relatively small moving targets such as capital ships.

The new superlaser and drive systems required larger power generators, which necessitated that the station would be much larger than its predecessor. When finished, the second Death Star would have over twice the volume of the original at 160 kilometers in diameter. To repel attacks from starfighters and capital ships, Lemelisk's plans included over 30,000 turbolasers, 7,500 laser cannons, and 5,000 ion cannons.

The second Death Star was constructed in orbit of the Forest Moon of Endor. Despite the improvements in the station's design, one flaw remained: the Emperor's hubris. His overconfidence allowed the forces of the Rebel Alliance to destroy the station, signaling a death knell for the Empire.

SPECIFICATIONS

CRAFT: **Death Star II battlestation**
MANUFACTURER: **Imperial Department**
  of Military Research
DIAMETER: **160km (99.4 miles)**
HYPERDRIVE: **Class 3.0**
HYPERDRIVE BACKUP: **20**
SHIELDING: **Equipped**
NAVIGATION SYSTEM: **Navicomputer**

ARMAMENT: **Superlaser, 15,000 turbolaser batteries, 15,000**
  heavy turbolasers, 7,500 laser cannons, 5,000 ion cannons,
  and 1,500 tractor-beam emplacements
CREW: **485,560; 152,275 gunners; 1,295,950 troops; 127,570**
  infantry; 75,860 technical personnel; 334,432 support ship
  pilots and crew
CARGO CAPACITY: **Over one million kilotons**
CONSUMABLES: **3 years**
COST: **Unknown**

Based on the design of Geonosian masticators used for the construction of Trade Federation battleships, Imperial Masticators are spherical vessels engineered to capture asteroids, break the asteroids down into raw materials, and prepare the processed materials for hull-plate extruders.

Each Imperial Masticator was equipped with tractor beam generators and projectors to draw asteroids into the maws of fusion-powered masticators. Masticators had maws with whirling durasteel teeth, which chewed the asteroid to tiny bits, and mixed the bits with alloy ores, including quadanium that had been mined and imported from the planet Despayre. Water was added to the resulting gravel, which was put under high pressure to form a semiliquid mixture that fed into pipelines that led to the smelters. Essentially huge melting pots that refined the mix, the smelters burned off impurities before the resulting scarified ore was conveyed to extruders that pressed out the hull plates. Leftover slag was gathered, then ejected toward the solar system's central star.

↓ **After gathering and processing raw materials from an asteroid belt, Imperial Masticators worked in tandem with hull-plate extruders to construct the battle station.**

Imperial Masticators not only processed materials, but were also equipped with large utility arms and docking arms, enabling them to work directly on the Death Star's superstructure.

Determined to fully utilize the Masticators, Bevel Lemelisk engineered them so that they could be relatively easily dismantled, and then separated into components that could be reformed and incorporated into the Death Star during the battle station's final stages of construction.

IMPERIAL HULL-PLATE EXTRUDERS (HPES)

Equipped with sublight engines, Imperial hull-plate extruders were orbital manufacturing facilites that created complex cross-sectional materials for Imperial Star Destroyers and other large spacecraft. The Death Star's designers programmed the extruders to produce broad, curved durasteel plating that would simultaneously support the station's surface structures and protect the subsurface levels.

AT-CT
(ALL TERRAIN CONSTRUCTION TRANSPORT)

Used for large-scale construction projects on distant worlds, single-pilot All Terrain Construction Transports have advanced tractor beam technology that can lift, manipulate, and move heavy objects with ease. Death Star construction crews used the vehicles to move girders, crates, and other pieces of heavy equipment to precise locations.

↘ Manufactured by Kuat Drive Yards under the direction of the Imperial Department of Military Research, the All Terrain Construction Transport incorporated technology and parts from the Imperial All Terrain Scout Transport. The pressurized cockpit allowed pilots to operate in airless environments.

➜ The large opening in the Death Star's superstructure allowed access for vehicles and droids during the battle station's construction.

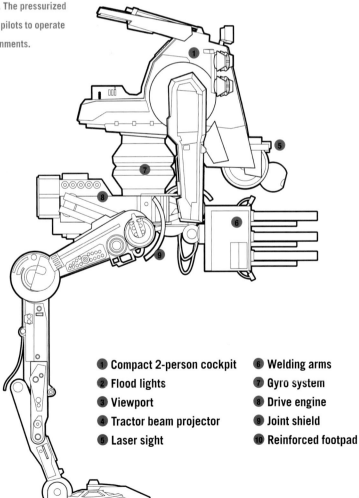

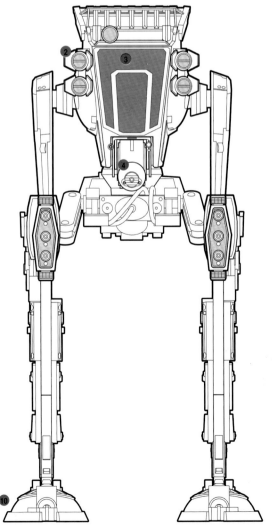

1. Compact 2-person cockpit
2. Flood lights
3. Viewport
4. Tractor beam projector
5. Laser sight
6. Welding arms
7. Gyro system
8. Drive engine
9. Joint shield
10. Reinforced footpad

PLANETARY SHIELD GENERATOR

Although the second Death Star, during its construction in orbit of the Forest Moon of Endor, was guarded by Imperial star destroyers and other warships, its most significant defense was a massive CoMar SLD-26 planetary shield generator. More powerful than any standard deflector shield system, a planetary shield is a force field that nullifies both physical and energy attacks. It uses layers of charged energy that are capable of not only dissipating turbolaser blasts and destroying space debris on contact, but is impervious to concussion missiles, asteroids, comet strikes, and enemy starships of any size. In fact, a collision with a planetary shield will reduce any starship to space dust.

Built on the forest moon's surface, the SLD-26 planetary shield generator consisted of a dish network, an underground generator, and an above-ground shield projector complex that spanned an area of 70km (43 miles) in diameter. The planetary shield generator projected an energy screen that completely enveloped the orbital Death Star II, and could be easily defended by anti-infantry and anti-vehicle turrets. The only

weapon capable of penetrating the energy screen was a superlaser.

Because the planetary shield generator's projected energy screen has great destructive power and is virtually invisible, it can be used as an offensive weapon. Enemy pilots are forced to rely on sensor readings to avoid contact with the energy screen, but technicians can jam or block enemy sensors to effectively conceal the planetary shield's presence. The Empire used this tactic at the Battle of Endor, and nearly destroyed numerous rebel starfighters.

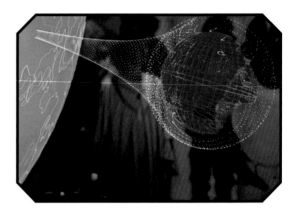

⬇ Constructed by Imperial forces on Endor, an elevated landing platform was the touch-down deck for Imperial shuttles and other spacecraft. The platform's columnar legs housed turbo lifts that led to corridors and catwalks that terminated at loading gantries for All Terrain Armored Transports (AT-ATs).

1. Emitter antenna
2. Amplification projector
3. Projection focusers
4. Shield projectors
5. Focus dish
6. Projector relay
7. Amplification grid
8. Project adjust
9. Capacitor banks
10. Power core
11. Turbine generator

← Stolen holographic schematics of the Imperial planetary shield generator allowed the Rebel Alliance to form a plan to destroy the second Death Star.

↓ Guarded by scout troopers, a reinforced durasteel-plated bunker served as a back door to the shield generator's control room and power generator.

↓ Located beneath Endor's surface, the Imperial installation's primary and back-up generators supplied power to the massive defensive shield projector.

THRONE ROOM

Built within an armored sphere on the uppermost level of a high tower on the Death Star, the Imperial throne room was a fully functional command center that allowed the Emperor to control, monitor, and communicate with all areas of the battle station. The throne used technologies tuned to the Emperor's unique physical and mental patterns, and responded only to his commands. Large windows offered expansive views of the station and surrounding space. The tower was the most heavily shielded portion of the entire battle station, and its hull was doubly reinforced to protect against incoming artillery, making the tower virtually impenetrable from the outside. In the event that the tower ever suffered structural damage, an emergency throne room was located within the armored sphere, just below the tower.

The main area of the throne room was split into three levels. A narrow overseer gantry stretched above the central floor , and was connected to a single turbolift shaft that ran the length of the tower. The lift shaft was situated inside a larger, open well that plunged for many kilometers, and led directly to the Death Star's main reactor core.

The royal living quarters and quarters for the Emperor's personal body guards were located below the throne room. When the throne room and royal apartment were unoccupied, four squads of stormtroopers guarded it in the Emperor's absence. When the Emperor was present, the stormtroopers were replaced by four squads of the Imperial Royal Guard.

To deter unwanted visitors, all corridors leading to the throne room and royal apartments were loaded with traps and security measures. Anyone approaching the corridor that led to the tower's restricted turbolift was required to punch in an identifying code before entering the trap-filled passageway. Those who failed to identify themselves properly were subject to either immediate capture or death by laserfire.

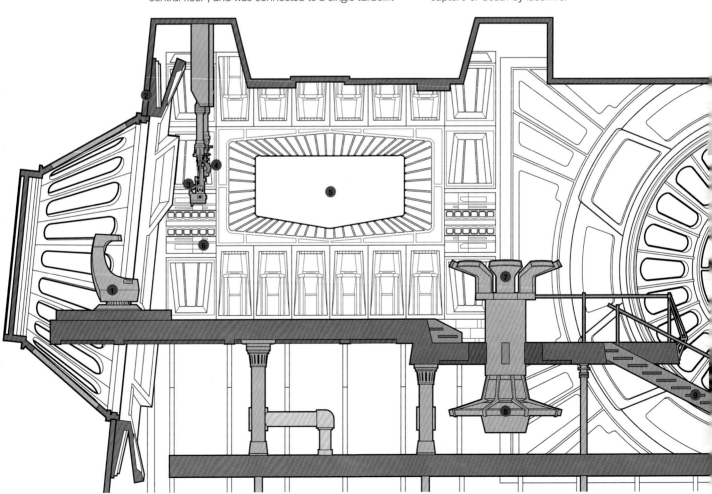

COMMAND SEAT

The Emperor's throne concealed a personal deflector shield generator and layers of ultra-dense alloyed armor. A panel on one of the armrests had controls that allowed the Emperor to turn the massive throne, and also light-beam secure communication links to summon members of the Imperial Guard, Darth Vader, the Death Star's commander, or the Emperor's advisors. Control consoles throughout the upper and lower levels of the throne room were engineered to allow a small staff of officers to override and operate all of the battle station's functions from the tower.

1. **Throne**
2. **Reinforced hull**
3. **Targeting viewer**
4. **Holocam/projector**
5. **Viewscreen**
6. **Display controls**
7. **Duty post**
8. **Lower console**
9. **Staircase**
10. **Catwalk**
11. **Transparasteel viewport**
12. **Bridge to turbolift**

↑ Emperor Palpatine surveyed his throne room from a swivel-mounted seat.

↓ Inside the shielded tower, the Emperor's Royal Guards were stationed by a turbolift.

SIZE COMPARISON CHART

Death Star II
(incomplete)

Torpedo Sphere

Death Star

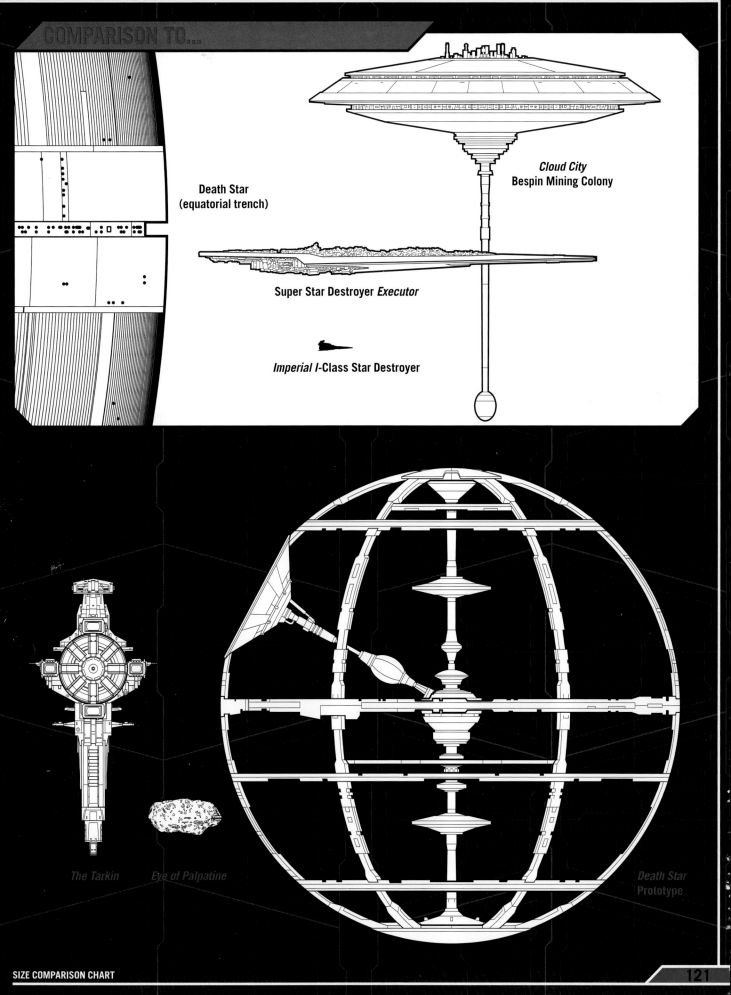

Death Star
(equatorial trench)

Cloud City
Bespin Mining Colony

Super Star Destroyer *Executor*

Imperial I-Class Star Destroyer

The Tarkin

Eye of Palpatine

Death Star
Prototype

ACKNOWLEDGMENTS

The author and artists of the *Death Star Owner's Workshop Manual* incorporated information about the Death Star from previously published *Star Wars* technical guides, game books, sourcebooks, and novels. We are especially indebted to Bill Slavicsek for his work on the invaluable *Star Wars: Death Star Technical Companion*. Other notable sources of reference include *The Star Wars Sourcebook* by Bill Slavicsek and Curtis Smith; *Star Wars Galaxy Guide 1: A New Hope* by Michael Stern and Paul Sudlow; *Star Wars Galaxy Guide 5: Return of the Jedi* by Michael Stern and George Strayton; *Star Wars: Imperial Sourcebook* by Greg Gorden; *Star Wars: The New Essential Guide to Characters* by Daniel Wallace; *Star Wars: The Essential Guide to Vehicles and Vessels* and *Star Wars: The Essential Guide to Weapons and Technology* by Bill Smith and Troy Vigil; *Star Wars Technical Journal* by Shane Johnson; *Star Wars: Incredible Cross-Sections: The Classic Trilogy* by David West Reynolds, Hans Jenssen, and Richard Chasemore; *The Complete Star Wars Encyclopedia* by Stephen J. Sansweet and Pablo Hidalgo with contributions from Bob Vitas, Daniel Wallace, Chris Cassidy, Mary Franklin, and Josh Kushins; *Star Wars: Death Star* by Michael Reeves and Steve Perry; and *Star Wars: The Blueprints* by J.W. Rinzler.

Special thanks to the following people for their help with reference for this project: Gus Lopez, Philip Wise, Michael Erwin, Daren Murrer, Cole Horton, Tiny Panganiban, Guy Vardaman, Zach Spencer, Marcus Thompson, Jean-François Boivin, and our friends at Lucasfilm including Leland Chee, Pablo Hidalgo, Stacey Leong, and Jonathan Rinzler.

We also gratefully acknowledge George Lucas, John Barry, Joe Johnston, Ralph McQuarrie, Lorne Peterson, Norman Reynolds, and their colleagues for their significant contributions to the Death Star in the *Star Wars* movies.

RYDER WINDHAM

A former editor for Dark Horse Comics, Ryder Windham is the author of more than fifty *Star Wars* books. His previous collaborations with artists Chris Trevas and Chris Reiff include *Star Wars Blueprints: The Ultimate Collection*, *Star Wars Blueprints: Rebel Edition*, *Star Wars: Millennium Falcon—A 3-D Owner's Guide* and the Haynes *Millennium Falcon Owner's Workshop Manual*. He resides with his family in Providence, Rhode Island.

CHRIS REIFF

Chris Reiff is an illustrator, toy designer, and inventor with more than 17 years experience working on official *Star Wars* projects and with licenses from companies like Marvel and Disney. Some of his latest illustration works include *The Bounty Hunter Code*, and *Star Wars Lightsaber Thumb Wrestling*. He lives in Cincinnati, Ohio with his dog named Dog and the full-size R2-D2 replica he built for himself.
www.chrisreiff.com

CHRIS TREVAS

Chris Trevas has been working professionally in the *Star Wars* universe since 1995 illustrating everything from limited edition fine art prints to floaty pens. His numerous book projects include *Star Wars: The Essential Reader's Companion* and *Darth Vader: A 3-D Reconstruction Log*. Chris works from his home studio in Beverly Hills, Michigan where he lives with his wife and three daughters.
www.christrevas.com

← "Battle for Death Star (fighters dive on sphere)" (1975) was artist Ralph McQuarrie's first concept painting of the Death Star for *Star Wars*. Although the painting is frequently inverted for publication, McQuarrie intended it to be viewed with this orientation.

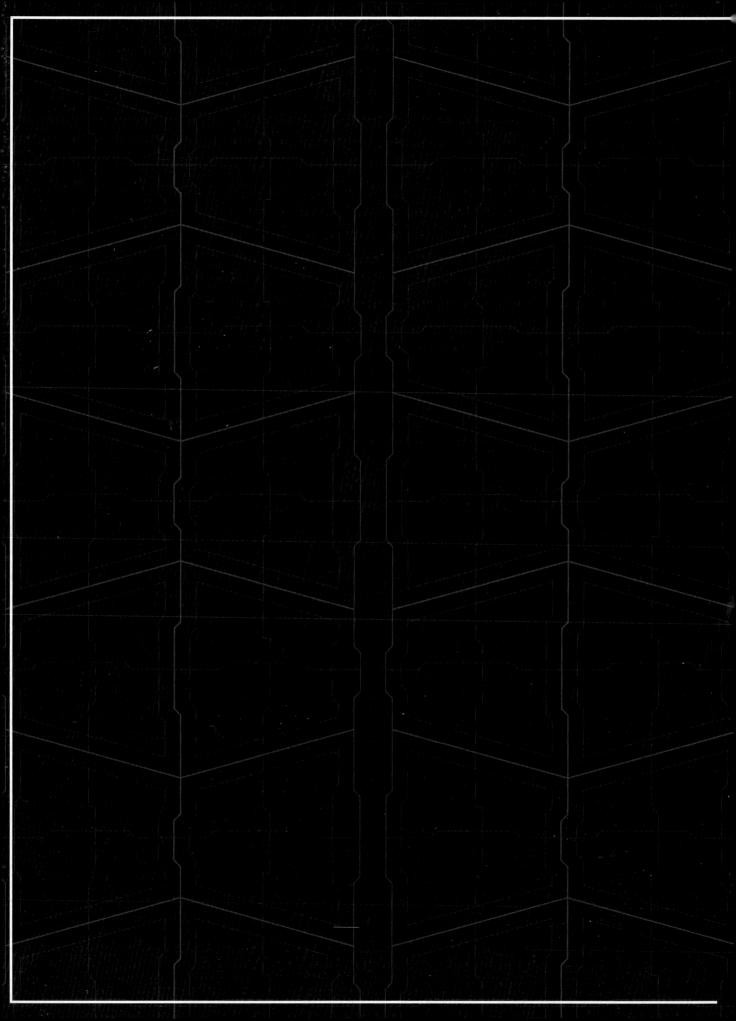